The DNA of the Nazarenes
A Core Course of the School of Leadership

Church of the Nazarene

Mesoamerica Region

Ruthie Córdova Carvallo

The DNA of the Nazarenes

A book in the "School of Leadership" series.
Core Level Course

Author: Ruthie Córdova Carvallo

Spanish Editor: Dr. Mónica E. Mastronardi de Fernández
Spanish Reviewer: Dr. Rubén Fernández
Translator: Alejandra Martínez de Riddell
Reviewer: Shelley J. Webb

Material produced by EDUCATION AND CLERGY DEVELOPMENT
of the Church of the Nazarene, Mesoamerica Region. www.edunaz.org
Mailing Address: PO Box 3977 - 1000 San José, Costa Rica, Central América.
Phone (506) 2285-0432 / 0423 - Email: EL@mesoamericaregion.org

Publisher and Distributor: Asociación Región Mesoamérica
Av. 12 de Octubre Plaza Victoria Locales 5 y 6
Pueblo Nuevo Hato Pintado, Ciudad de Panamá
Tel. (507) 203-3541
E-mail: literatura@mesoamericaregion.org

Copyright © 2017 - All rights reserved.
Reproduction whole or in part, by any means, without written permission from
Education and Clergy Development of the Church of the Nazarene, Mesoamerica Region is prohibited.
www.mesoamericaregion.org

All Biblical quotations are from the New International Version-2011, unless otherwise noted.

Design: Juan Manuel Fernandez (www.juanfernandez.ga)
Cover image: Joshua Jordan
Cover images and interiors of the covers used with permission under license by Creative Commons.

Digital printing

Table of Contents

Lesson 1	Our Identity	9
Lesson 2	Our Origins	17
Lesson 3	Our Founder	25
Lesson 4	Our History	33
Lesson 5	Our Beliefs	41
Lesson 6	Our Organization	49
Lesson 7	Our Values and Mission	57
Lesson 8	Our Lifestyle	65

Introduction

The book series **School of Leadership** is designed with the purpose of providing a tool to the church for formation, education and training of its members to actively integrate into Christian service the gifts and calling (vocation) they have received from the Lord.

Each book provides study materials for one course in the **School of Leadership** program offered by the theological Institutions of the Mesoamerica Region of the Church of the Nazarene. These institutions include: IBN (Coban, Guatemala); STN (Guatemala City); SENAMEX (Mexico City); SENDAS (San Jose, Costa Rica); SND (Santo Domingo, Dominican Republic); and SETENAC (Havana, Cuba). A number of leaders from these schools (presidents, directors, vice presidents and directors of decentralized academic studies) actively participated in the program design.

The **School of Leadership** has five core courses that are common to all ministries, and six specialized courses for each ministry area, at the end of which, the respective theological institution awards the student a certificate (or diploma) in Specialized Ministry.

The overall objective of the **School of Leadership** is "to work with the local church in equipping the saints for the work of the ministry establishing a solid biblical and theological foundation and developing them through the practice of exercising their gifts for service in the local congregation and society as a whole." The specific objectives of this program are threefold:

- Develop the ministerial gifts of the local congregation.
- Multiply service ministries in the church and community.
- Raise awareness of the vocation of professional ministry in its diverse forms.

We thank Dr. Monica Mastronardi de Fernandez for her dedication as General Editor of the project, and the Regional Coordinators of Ministries and the team of writers and designers who collaborated to publish these books. We are equally grateful to the teachers who will share these materials. They will make a difference in the lives of thousands of people in the Mesoamerica Region and beyond.

Finally, we thank Dr. L. Carlos Saenz, Mesoamerica Regional Director, for his continued support in this work, which is the result of his conviction that the church must be holistically equipped.

We pray for God's blessing for all the disciples whose lives and Christian service will be enriched by these books.

Dr. Ruben E. Fernandez
Theological Education Coordinator
Mesoamerica Region

What is the School of Leadership?

The **School of Leadership** is an educational program for lay ministry in different specialties to engage in the mission of the local church. This program is administered by the Theological Institutions of the Church of the Nazarene in the Mesoamerica Region and taught both at these institutions and in the local churches enrolled in the program.

Who can Benefit from the School of Leadership?

It is for all the members of the Church of the Nazarene who have participated in Levels B and C of the discipleship program, and who, with all their heart, wish to discover their gifts and serve God in His work.

The Plan ABCDE

In order to contribute to the formation of the members of their churches, the Church of the Nazarene in the Mesoamerica Region has adopted the plan of discipleship ABCDE, and since 2001 began publishing materials for each of these levels. The School of Leadership is Level D of the ABCDE discipleship plan and is designed for those who have been through previous levels of discipleship.

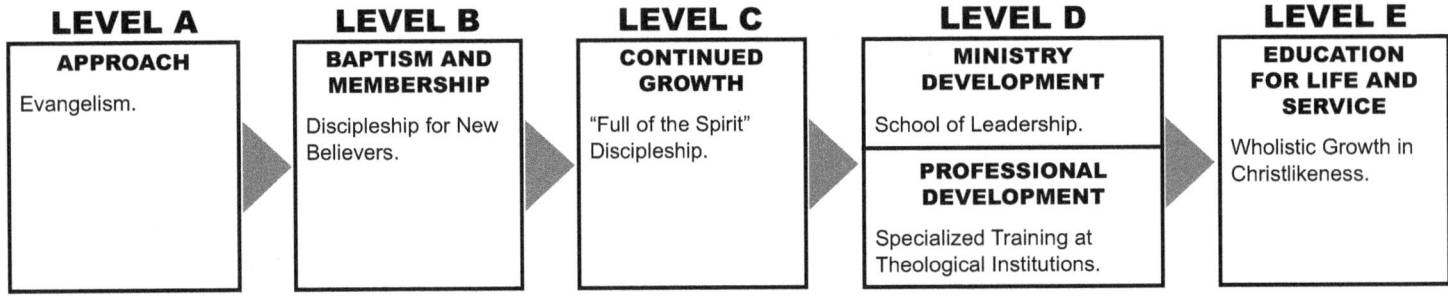

In the Church of the Nazarene, we believe making disciples in the image of Christ in the nations is the foundation of missionary work and the responsibility of leadership (Ephesians 4: 7-16). The work of discipleship is continuous and dynamic; therefore, the disciple never stops growing in the likeness of his Lord. This growth, when healthy, occurs in all dimensions: the individual dimension (spiritual growth), the corporate dimension (joining the congregation), the holiness in life dimension (progressive transformation of our being and doing according to model of Jesus Christ) and the service dimension (investing our lives in ministry).

Dr. Monica Mastronardi de Fernandez
Managing Editor, The School of Leadership Book Series

How do I Use this Book?

This book contains eight lessons of the School of Leadership program, along with activities and final evaluation of the course.

How are the contents of this book organized?

Each of the eight lessons of this book contains the following:

> **Objectives:** These are the learning objectives the student is expected to understand at the end of the lesson.

> **Main Ideas:** A summary of the key teachings of the lesson.

> **Development of Lesson:** This is the largest section because it is the development of the contents of the lesson. The lessons have been written so that the book can be the teacher, and for that reason the contents have been written in a dynamic form and in simple language with contemporary ideas.

> **Notes and Comments:** The information in the margins is intended to clarify terms and provide notes that complement or extend the content of the lesson.

> **Questions:** Sometimes questions are included in the margin that the teacher can use to introduce or reinforce a lesson topic.

> **What did we learn?:** The box at the end of the lesson development section provides a brief summary of the lesson.

> **Activities:** This is a page at the end of each lesson that contains learning activities, for individuals or groups, on the subject studied. The estimated time for implementation in class is 20 minutes.

> **Final evaluation of the course:** This is the last page of the book and once completed the student must remove it from the book and hand it in to a course instructor. The final evaluation should take about 15 minutes.

How long is each course?

The courses are designed for 12 hours of class over 8 ninety-minute sessions. Each institution and each church or local theological study center will coordinate days and times of the classes. Within this hour and a half the teacher or the teachers should include time for the activities contained in the book.

What is the role of the student?

The student is responsible for the following:

1. Enroll on time for the course.
2. Buy the book and study each lesson before class time.
3. Arrive for class on time.
4. Participate in class activities.
5. Participate in practical ministry in the local church outside of class.
6. Complete and submit the final evaluation to the teacher.

What is the role of the teacher of the course?

The professors and teachers for the School of Leadership courses are pastors and laity committed to the mission and ministry of the church and preferably have experience in the ministry they teach. The Director and/or the School of Leadership at the local church (or theological institution) invites their participation and their functions are the following:

1. Be well prepared by studying the book's content and scheduling the use of class time. When studying the lesson, you should have on hand the Bible and a dictionary. Although the lessons are written using simple language, it is recommended that you "translate" what you consider difficult in order to help the students understand. In other words, use terms that they can better understand.

2. Ensure that the students are studying the material in the book and achieving the learning objectives.

3. Plan and accompany students in the activities of ministerial practice. The local pastor and the director of the respective ministry must schedule these activities. These activities should not take away from class time.

4. Take daily attendance and grades in the class report form. The final average will be the result demonstrated by the student in the following activities:

   a. Class work

   b. Participation in ministerial practice outside of class

   c. Final evaluation

5. At the end of the course, collect the evaluation sheets and hand them in with the form "Class Report" to the local School of Leadership director. Do this after totaling the averages and verifying that all data is complete on the form.

6. Professors and teachers should not add tasks or reading assignments apart from the contents of the book. They should be creative in the design of the learning activities and in planning ministry activities outside the classroom according to the reality of their local church and its context.

How do I teach a class?

We recommend using a 90-minute class session as follows:

- **5 minutes:** Review the topic of the previous lesson and pray together.

- **30 minutes:** Review and discuss the lesson. We recommend using an outline, chalkboard, cardboard or other available materials, using dynamic learning activities and visual media such as graphics, drawings, objects, pictures, questions, assigning students to submit parts of the lesson, and so on. We do not recommend lecturing or having the teacher reread the lesson content.

- **5 minutes:** Break either in the middle of class or when it is convenient.

- **20 minutes:** Work on activities in the book. This can be done at the beginning, middle or end of the review, or you can complete the activities as you proceed in accordance with the issues as it relates to them.

• **20 minutes:** Discussion about the students' ministry practice that they currently do and that they will do. At the beginning of the course you will need to present the schedule to the students so that they can make arrangements to attend the ministry practice. In the classes when the students discuss their ministry practice, the conversation should be focused on what they learned, including their successes and their errors, as well as the difficulties they encountered.

• **10 minutes:** Prayer for the issues arising from the practice (challenges, people, problems, goals, gratitude for the results, among others).

How do I implement the final course evaluation?

Allocate 15 minutes of time during the last class meeting for the course evaluation. If necessary, students may consult their books and Bibles. Final evaluations are designed to be an activity to reinforce what was learned in class and not a repetition of the contents of the book. The purpose of this assessment is to measure the understanding and evaluation of the student concerning the class topics, their spiritual growth, their progress in the commitment to the mission of the church and their progress in ministerial experience.

Ministerial Practice Activities

The following are suggested activities for ministerial practice outside of class. The list below includes several ideas to help teachers, pastors, directors of local School of Leadership groups and local ministry directors. From the list you can choose the activity best suited to the contextual situation and the local church ministry, or replace these with others according to the needs and possibilities of your context.

We recommend having at least three ministerial activities per course. You can put the whole class to work on a project or assign group tasks according to interests, gifts and abilities. It is advisable to involve students in a variety of new ministry experiences.

Suggested Ministry Activities for The DNA of the Nazarenes

1. Have students form a working committee to organize a worship service or special event to celebrate the anniversary of the Church of the Nazarene in the month of October.

2. Coordinate with church cell groups, discipleship groups, Sunday School classes, youth groups, or other group meetings to give a lecture on the history of our founders or other subjects studied.

3. Have students prepare a special pamphlet or handout on the history of the denomination.

4. Have students prepare a visual art to teach the values of the Church of the Nazarene (such as bookmarks, banners, video presentations, etc.).

5. Have students prepare a drama or three short dramas for one or more church services outlining the position of the denomination in terms of some critical issues in the contemporary context.

6. Have students teach the children about the values of the church using puppets, clowns, mimes, dramas or other creative means according to their gifts and abilities.

7. Have the students visit homes in the community to talk to the neighbors about the values of the church and to invite them to a special evangelistic meeting.

8. Have students organize a special event or thanksgiving worship service on the birthday of the local church where each family brings a gift for use in ministry (ex: Bibles, supplies for children's classes, decorations for the building, construction needs, needs of the parsonage, supplies for the worship team, etc.). These activities work best when a list of needs is provided.

Lesson 1

Our Identity

Objectives

- To know our denominational identity.
- To embrace the denominational identity in the local church.
- To express our denominational identity.

Main Ideas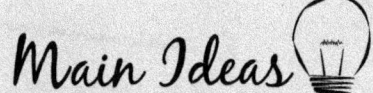

- Identity is something that we have in common with a group that makes the group unique and different from others.
- The denominational identity is based on a combination of purposes, beliefs and values of a Christian community.

Introduction

Each person has unique, inherited physical traits in their genes that are contained in the DNA. The acronym DNA is the abbreviation for "deoxyribonucleic acid." This acid dwells in the nuclei of all living cells and functions as a tiny computer chip since it contains the genetic information that the body will use to guide development and functioning. The DNA is responsible for transmitting the rich inheritance of our ancestors and makes up our identity.

What Is Identity?

In this section we will learn the significance of the word identity.

The Manual of the Church of the Nazarene is revised and updated by the General Assembly of the Church of the Nazarene every four years. We recommend that you consult the latest version of the Manual as you study this course.
The website for the downloadable manual can be found in the bibliography.

Each person acquires an identity that begins with his or her genetics and is formed throughout life by the influence of family, customs, country, sex, name, and society, among others. Identity is a set of characteristics that makes someone or something recognizable without confusion with another. Identity is what distinguishes us as belonging to a family or group of people. Thus, it is said that when a person has identity the person is consistent with who they are and in what they do and this does not change, no matter the circumstances.

In society, institutions, companies and organizations also have identities that characterize them. These entities create, form and maintain what is known as corporate identity, which is the way in which their values, promises, beliefs, behaviors and levels of satisfaction are transmitted. That identity is formed and strengthened, first, by everyone who works in that company or institution, from the members of the executive board to the workers in the organization. Secondly, the organizations spend time, use resources and invest large amounts of money to create and care for the corporate identity to make an impact that will result in significant benefits for the company.

As a Christian organization, the Church of the Nazarene also has a distinct identity that characterizes it and which is expressed in its mission, beliefs and values. An aspect of this identity is being part of the universal Church of Jesus Christ.

In the New Testament, every local church is part of the universal Church, and every person who is a member of the local church is a member of the universal Church of Jesus Christ. A local church is visible, but the universal Church is invisible, being composed of believers of all generations, who are not present in bodily form, but are part of the Church that Jesus Christ will come to seek, in His second coming (1 Thessalonians 4:13-17).

The Bible teaches there is only one Church, the Church of Jesus Christ. Not everything that today uses the term "church" has a Biblical foundation. The true nature of the Church has a double identity: a people brought out of the world by God to worship Him and sent back to the world to witness and serve.

Another aspect of the identity of the Church of the Nazarene, is that it begins with the story of the people of God found in the Old and New Testaments. It is a church that accepts the Christian creeds, is considered Protestant in a doctrinal sense, and is a Wesleyan church, historically identified with a particular theological tradition: Methodism, and is promoted as a holiness church.

The mission, values, beliefs and other aspects make up a "church culture" that identifies the members of our denomination anywhere in the world.

> A definition of the church: "The church is *local* and *universal*: i.e., it is a definite group of believers meeting in one place, yet it also is the totality of all believers everywhere in every generation" (Taylor, 114).

Why Is it Important to Have an Identity?

In this section, we will study about the value of having an identity.

Having an identity is very valuable and important. On a personal level, identity is inherited, modeled, formed and strengthened throughout life.

Christians also develop an identity as followers of Jesus Christ, as members of a local church and part of the universal Church. This identity gives a sense of belonging, purpose for life and a clearly defined mission.

It is very important to have a Christian identity amidst a backdrop of religious confusion. It is the hope that this identity will provide roots that give support, stability, security, a sense of belonging, and establish benchmarks or parameters for making decisions.

Identity, in a sense, is received as an inheritance, and it is necessary to know, understand, evaluate and maintain it. Dr. John Knight, who was the 25th General Superintendent of the denomination, studied the First Letter to the Corinthians, chapter 15:1-4 and noted three important ideas of the Apostle Paul on Christian identity:

> *Methodism: The church founded by John Wesley, characterized by prayer, Bible study, social work, and the preaching of the holy life, among other things, using particular strategies in the formation of new Christians.*

Lesson 1 - Our Identity

First of all, that the education that has been received (tradition) should be retained and considered as a living legacy. Secondly, we have a responsibility to take those lessons and pass them on as an inheritance to be others. Thirdly, these teachings should be centered on Jesus Christ who is the pure gospel, and for this reason it is a "Christological" inheritance (Knight: 15-16).

Christology: The study of theology that deals with different aspects of the person of Christ as the Savior of the world.

So, every Nazarene has a personal heritage that has been received from the denomination and the Wesleyan Holiness movement, and we are obligated to pass it on to the next generation, but above all, we are obligated to keep the tradition alive (truths, teachings of the Gospel of Christ) and strengthen unity and fellowship.

However, if the tradition is not kept alive, there is a danger of it being lost. Dr. Knight writes that this happens when what you receive and learn (doctrine) becomes only a formula that is repeated, when the practices become rituals and when the beliefs lose their significance. Dr. Knight also mentions there is a danger of losing the tradition when the evangelical message loses its central place and is replaced by less important things and when worship becomes impersonal in place of a vital relationship with the living and holy God.

What Are the Components of the Nazarene Identity?

Now we will learn the five components of our identity.

The heritage of the Church of the Nazarene is characterized by several elements that become components of its identity. For Dr. Knight, these key elements are loyalty to the Word of God as the only source of authority for our beliefs and practices in the Christian faith; the emphasis on the doctrine of entire sanctification; biblical preaching; the spirit of spontaneity in worship and music; evangelism; missions; compassion; Christian education and theology; youth; and the leadership of the denomination under the guidance of superintendents. All these elements have contributed to the formation and permanence of the denomination through the years.

As in the identity of a person or organization, these aspects are part of our denominational identity: values, a name, traditions, history, organization, commitment, a sense of belonging, culture, beliefs, etc. Therefore, to better know and understand the Church of the Nazarene as a denomination, it is important to understand its founders, its background as a Christian church in the Wesleyan tradition, its genealogy, origins, beliefs, teachings, mission, values and unique characteristics; that is to say, it is important to understand its identity within the theological diversity of the world.

The Church of the Nazarene around the world shares five key components that support the denominational identity. They are the following: history, theology, organization, mission and lifestyle.

The history includes the origins of the name, characteristics and distinctions, its founding leaders, their vision, their challenges, their first convictions, the church's relationship with sister denominations, etc.

The theology includes the beliefs of the denomination, its doctrinal foundations, tradition or theological identity, its emphasis, its teachings, its differences with other theological traditions, etc.

The organization reveals the polity of the denomination, its purpose, its structures, its ministries, its goals, and its administration in different areas.

The mission guides the denomination, and includes the nature of its calling, the vision, task, scope, and development of the church.

The lifestyle is established by the Christian experience of its members and is a result of their obedience to live a holy life which is manifested in their Christian character and conduct, in their values, their worldview, and in their position on moral and contemporary social issues, all of which leads them to be more like Jesus Christ.

Our Evangelical Identity

In this section we will learn about our evangelical heritage.

The Rev. Wilfredo Canales explains that we are an evangelical church with a well-defined legacy. Our church is rooted in a rich Christian history. Therefore, we consider ourselves heirs of an evangelical legacy that is connected to the preaching of our Lord Jesus Christ. The Articles of Faith of our Constitution give the best testimony of the "deposit that has been entrusted to you," using the words of Paul. These are not simply doctrinal statements without living roots. Rather, they are a constant reminder of the inner life which must move us to fulfill the mission.

The evangelical identity that characterizes our church springs from a deep commitment to Scripture as our ultimate standard of faith and behavior. Within this evangelical heritage, we take on, with integrity, the Biblical message of the life of holiness as the standard for a Christian faith that honors God and seeks to be useful for His purposes.

We need to relate Biblical teaching with the problematic environment in which the church ministers. There should be no area of the human condition that is excluded from the proclamation and influence of the total salvation message of God in Christ Jesus.

How Is Our Nazarene Identity Formed and Strengthened in the Local Church?

Here we will learn how to preserve and convey our identity.

Legacy: Anything handed dow from the past. as from an ancestor or predecessor.

Some local churches may have families that have been Nazarenes for many years. In this case, it is gratifying to know that they are trying to preserve the identity of the church, reading missionary stories, supporting

Lesson 1 - Our Identity

the celebrations of anniversaries and events in the denomination and local church, being faithful in attendance at activities and church services for both the local church and the district, being generous to fund projects of any kind that the church sponsors at local, district or international levels and enthusiastically sharing the gospel and the message of holiness with others.

In the case of members who come from different churches or who have no religious background, it is important to work with them to instill a sense of identity. This can be done through membership classes, reading clubs on the history of the denomination and by encouraging participation in the anniversary celebrations and festivities of the local church, the anniversary of the denomination, and special days (Pastor Appreciation Day, John Wesley Day, the day of Phineas Bresee, etc.). Also, the church can encourage new Nazarenes to attend denominational events at the district, national and international levels (conferences, meetings, retreats, conferences, etc.) so they can contribute their ideas and suggestions and in doing so, foster a love for the church.

Each local church needs a permanent plan to intentionally disciple the new converts and members with the teaching of the distinctive beliefs and traditions of the Church of the Nazarene. The church should organize courses for baptism, membership, growth in holiness, ministry, leadership, etc.

It is necessary to teach new Christians not only the core beliefs common to all Christian churches, but also about the Nazarenes and Wesleyans. One option is to conduct discussion groups to talk to members of the local church about what it means to be Nazarene and Wesleyan, referring to the historical and theological perspective and the differences with other traditions.

It is equally valuable to promote the educational materials of the denomination. Dedicate a weekend to introduce the members of the local church to what the church offers for the formation and spiritual growth at different ages, from materials on evangelism to theological training. Show how to use materials creatively, on the individual level, the family level, in small groups and in Sunday School classes.

Likewise, promote denominational missionary programs through creative and engaging activities that capture the interest, broaden the vision, generate motivation and stimulate involvement to support the mission. It is important that members feel that they participate in the overall mission of the denomination.

Good Biblical preaching strengthens denominational identity, especially when the sermons are expository, soundly based on theology, and designed to strengthen those practical teachings about holiness.

Another way to maintain the identity of the local church is to foster a sense of community where people connect with God and each other

Good Biblical preaching strangthens denominational identity.

and where they feel they are together as brothers in Christ by singing, praying, participating in the sacraments, supporting each other, and seeing themselves as part of a big, international family.

In summary, in order for a local church to create, train and maintain a strong denominational identity, it needs to take advantage of the available resources to help its members know and appreciate the strengths of the historical past of the Nazarenes, the Wesleyan theological identity, and its distinction as a holiness church. Also, it is important to maintain the doctrine of the church, the practices, worship emphasis and preaching. This can be done by investing time and resources in the discipleship of new converts; training and developing laity to use their gifts, abilities and talents in the work; and equipping the new converts for service to fulfill the mission of the church.

Having a denominational identity fosters in members a sense of belonging and facilitates the use of resources and efforts, thus benefiting the church everywhere in the world. However, if one or more aspects are neglected in the formation of identity, the local church is in danger of losing it. It is important to be alert and watch for signs that may damage or lead to loss of denominational identity, for example, if someone introduces beliefs, practices or other elements that are incompatible with doctrinal tradition.

What Did We Learn?

The Church of the Nazarene has a definite identity contained in five main components that are common to all Nazarenes throughout the world. It is important that the local church forms and maintains its identity.

Activities

Time 20'

INSTRUCTIONS:

1. Applying principles for organizations from Warren Bennis and Burt Nanus (Leaders: The Four Keys to Effective Leadership p. 35, 1994), we can state that a local church needs to safeguard their denominational identity. This will allow the church to be integral, that is to say, "having a sense of who they are and what they should do." In order to evaluate how much of this is true for your congregation, complete the following survey with 10 people:

    Why are you Nazarene?

    What is the distinctive doctrine of the Church of the Nazarene?

    Can you mention its founder?

    What is the mission of the denomination?

2. Write a list of six characteristics that describe your local church. What kind of church is it? Analyze and reflect on what you wrote in light of what is taught in this lesson on denominational identity.

_____ _____ _____
_____ _____ _____
_____
_____

3. Give 5 practical ways your church can form and strengthen its denominational identity.

_____
_____
_____
_____

4. Give 3 practical ideas that you and your family can do to form and strengthen your identity as Nazarenes.

_____
_____
_____

5. Think and write about 5 things that identify you as a Nazarene.

_____
_____
_____

Lesson 2

OUR ORIGIN

Objectives
- Understand that the Church of the Nazarene is a Christian church.
- Understand the nature and mission of the Christian Church.
- Appreciate the Biblical metaphors of the Church.

Main Ideas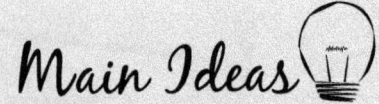
- The Church of Jesus Christ includes all who confess Jesus Christ as Lord and Savior.
- The Church of the Nazarene is part of the universal Christian Church because it confesses and proclaims Jesus Christ.

Ecumenical creeds:
A creed is a statement of the fundamental beliefs of the Christian church. In the early centuries, there were ecumenical councils at Nicaea (325) and Constantinople (381) where the councils summarized the teachings of the apostles in creeds, one of which is known as the Apostles' Creed. Since it dates from the first century, it is commonly used in the Catholic Church, the Orthodox Church and the Protestant Church. A copy of this creed is included in Lesson 5.

The Manual of the Church of the Nazarene
is a guide that contains, in an orderly and systematic form, information about the history, beliefs, organization, government, objectives, functions, procedures, mission, values, ethical practices, and official positions of the denomination. It is a tool of administrative support for church leadership and an effective tool in the work of the denomination.

Introduction

Being clear in our identity as Nazarenes enables us to establish who we are as a church and define our mission. In order to have a strong identity, it is necessary to reflect on the origin of the church and the nature of our mission in the world. Therefore, understanding what the church is and what it means to be the people of God and a community of believers is fundamental in order to have a vision of ministry that is effective and faithful to the gospel of Christ.

The Church of the Nazarene is part of the universal Church of Christ, which confesses Jesus Christ as Savior and Lord. It is based on Scripture as the Word of God and affirms the great historic ecumenical creeds of the Christian faith. Although there are some aspects that distinguish us as a denomination, as Nazarenes we identify ourselves as Christians along with the rest of the Christian churches past and present.

What Is a Christian Church?

In this section we will learn that the Church of the Nazarene is a Christian Church.

God himself instituted the Christian Church or the Church of Jesus Christ since it was Jesus Christ, and only Jesus, who gave his own life to save us from sin. Without Christ, there would be no Church. He is the founder and the foundation. The Church belongs to Him and not to us.

The Church is the "assembly of the called" (ecclesia). It is God who calls and saves, and those who respond to that call become adopted children of God. The Church was born on the day of Pentecost when the Holy Spirit was poured into the hearts of all who believed in Jesus. They received and accepted him as Savior and Lord and decided to follow him. The universal Church is made up of the children of God, who are Holy Spirit filled people, so that the individual church, rather than being an organization, is a living organism. Every Christian is a member of this family, which means that every Christian belongs to Christ's Church, also called the universal Church. So if we want to be loyal to Jesus Christ, we must be loyal to the Church.

The Church of the Nazarene states in its Manual that it considers itself a Christian church and this is expressed in several of its paragraphs. In Part II of the Constitution of the Church it is written:

> *23. The Church of God is composed of all spiritually regenerate persons, whose names are written in heaven.*
>
> *24. The churches severally are to be composed of such regenerate persons as by providential permission, and by the leadings of the Holy Spirit, become associated together for holy fellowship and ministries.*
>
> *25. The Church of the Nazarene is composed of those persons who have voluntarily associated themselves together according to the doctrines and polity of said church, and who seek holy Christian fellowship, the conversion of sinners, the entire sanctification of believers, their upbuilding in holiness, and the simplicity and spiritual power manifest in the primitive New Testament Church, together with the preaching of the gospel to every creature.*

Article of Faith XI summarizes what we believe about the church:

> *We believe in the Church, the community that confesses Jesus Christ as Lord, the covenant people of God made new in Christ, the Body of Christ called together by the Holy Spirit through the Word.*
>
> *God calls the Church to express its life in the unity and fellowship of the Spirit; in worship through the preaching of the Word, observance of the sacraments, and ministry in His name; by obedience to Christ, holy living, and mutual accountability.*
>
> *The mission of the Church in the world is to share in the redemptive and reconciling ministry of Christ in the power of the Spirit [through holy living, evangelism, discipleship, and service]. The Church fulfills its mission by making disciples through evangelism, education, showing compassion, working for justice, and bearing witness to the kingdom of God.*
>
> *The Church is a historical reality, which organizes itself in culturally conditioned forms; exists both as local congregations and as a universal body; sets apart persons called of God for specific ministries. God calls the Church to live under His rule in anticipation of the consummation at the coming of our Lord Jesus Christ.*

One of the essential values of the Church of the Nazarene is that <u>we are a church, a Christian people, and by this we mean that we are united with all believers in proclaiming the Lordship of Jesus Christ</u>. We preach love and God's forgiveness; we reflect God's character in church and community. We believe and accept the Scriptures as the sole source of authority, and we affirm the ecumenical creeds and beliefs of the Christian faith.

Who makes up the Church of the Nazarene?

The Reformation: the name given to the religious movement that occurred in Europe in the sixteenth century when several priests, intellectuals and political leaders denounced the abuses that were occurring within the Roman Catholic Church with the intention of renewing it spiritually. But a division occurred, and from this division arose Protestant Churches supported by several countries' governments such as Germany, England, France, Holland, Switzerland, Scotland, and Belgium, among others.

Lesson 2 - Our Origin

The Church is ONE
In the Church of Christ no one should be segregated or disparaged for issues of gender, race, culture, social status, education or other reasons (1 Corinthians 12-13-25). These harmonious relations in the church do not happen miraculously. Paul says in Ephesians 4:16 that the body must be "held together." The meaning of this Greek word sunarmologoumenon, is "set" or "tied" and results from the union of two words: sun and harmologos which means "binding" and "articulation." This figure illustrates the relationships of mutual help and solidarity that should exist between church members (Archibald Thomas Robertson).

Builders of the Church
Leaders must be good stewards of the human resources of the church. The figure of a building in 1 Corinthians 3:10-17 teaches that it is the responsibility of leaders to choose the right materials to assemble the pieces of the building so that each meets its particular function. Training and placing each person to work in the ministries for which he or she has been called is one of the main functions of Christian leadership.

Our denomination is also considered Christian because we are heirs of the early Protestant Reformation movement and because our historical roots, through the Methodist Church (John Wesley), lead us to be like the Christian church of the New Testament.

On the other hand, we understand that being a Christian is to be automatically a member of Christ's Church. You cannot live a Christian life outside a community of believers because that is where growth occurs, where we encourage each other, where the people work together and where we express God's love in relationships. We believe that you cannot live the life of holiness in isolation. It is in coexistence that we learn from each other and build the holy character of believers.

Biblical Images of the Church

Now we will learn more about the Church through Biblical metaphors.

The Body of Christ

The apostle Paul uses the metaphor of the Church as the body of Christ to teach about church unity and its purpose in this world. Paul has a fondness for the metaphor of the body, as it is very useful for teaching some of the features that make Christ's church unique among all other human associations.

Paul writes, *"Now you are the body of Christ, and each one of you is a part of it"* (1 Corinthians 12:27). In other words, what the apostle wishes to emphasize is not that the church looks like the body of Christ, but that the church is the body of Christ on earth. Richard Taylor comments that the term body of Christ *"is used to indicate the whole community of Christians which constitutes the extension of our Lord's earthly incarnation"* (Taylor, p. 81). When the church serves the world as Christ served, people can see Christ through the work of the church.

Other passages where Paul reinforces this truth are these:

a) Christ acts through the Church, His body (Ephesians 1:22-23).

b) Each member who joins the church is a part of the body of Christ (Ephesians 5:29-30).

c) Each member has a role and place in the body of Christ and this function or ministry should be a continuation of the work of Christ (1 Corinthians 12:12).

The Church of Christ of which the apostle speaks is the universal Church. Peter Larson explained that the bond that unites the Church is spiritual (Colossians 1:18, 24); it is the same Spirit of God that dwells in each of its members (1 Corinthians 1:13) and this Spirit is one, as Christ is one and cannot be divided. The Church is "one," because there is only one body. This unity expresses harmony, teamwork and working together to achieve common goals. The Church must be subject to Christ who is the head of the body. He is your Savior. Christ's Church has a body of believers in each "local church," but also has a body in the universal Church, composed of all the Christian churches of all cultures.

As a Building

In the New Testament, the redeemed are compared to a building. Some people today use the terms "church" (meaning the building) and "Church" (meaning the people of God) as synonyms. The word "Church" in the New Testament, explains Donald Kammerdiener, always refers to all men and women who are disciples of Christ (2 Corinthians 6:16) and never to a building where Christians gathered.

In Ephesians 2:19-22, the apostle Paul links the Church with a building whose foundation is the apostles and prophets, and whose cornerstone, which holds together all the construction, is Christ. This building is a holy temple and dwelling place of God in the Spirit. William Barclay warns of the dangers of basing the unity of the church on the organization, form of worship, rituals or the like.

The church is a building in continuous growth. The stones that form the structure of this building are the disciples of Christ (1 Peter 2:5). The true church continually strives to add new believers, which in turn become well grounded in the structure of the building and can support the others who will be added. In 1 Corinthians 14:12, Paul says that God gives spiritual gifts to the church members so they can build each other up. Each of the believers will be judged and rewarded on the day of reckoning on the basis of the excellence with which they have served using the gifts they were given (1 Corinthians 4:2).

As the Family of God

In Ephesians 2:19, the apostle Paul says that all Christians are members of the family of God. This is the same thing the apostle Peter referred to when he stated that Christians are from the same lineage (1 Peter 2:9-10). He is writing to believers and claiming that they are the "family of God." Just as God chose Israel to be his holy people among all peoples, so the Church has been chosen to be his special family.

The church is a family in training. Orlando Costas states that the church family exists as a result of tireless and unceasing love of the Father, and He formed the church to be the "first of the new creation," created to be an instrument of the Father in the dissemination of his love. The church is not a finished product, but a family in training whose members are learning to relate to each other in responsible ways.

The members of the family of God have much more in common that unites them than separates them. The ties that bind Christians are eternal truths that no human power or demonic power can destroy. Often, the issues that separate and create enmity between them are negligible when compared

Lineage
The word "lineage" means binding to a family by ties of blood. All who have accepted Christ as their Lord and Savior belong to the lineage of the family of God. The children of God are those who have been washed in the blood of the Lamb and have begun to live a new life under the will of God. The apostle Peter says that Christians are the "family of God."

Who is the Stone?
Peter agrees with Paul that Christ is the "living Stone" or "Chief Cornerstone" that holds up the building of the church (1 Peter 2: 4-8). Passages like this show that the assertion of the Roman Catholic Church that Peter is the cornerstone on which the church is built is not correct and is based on a mistaken interpretation of Matthew 16:18 (see also 1 Corinthians 3:11).

A Family in Training
Just as God chose Israel to be his holy people among other peoples, so also the Church has been chosen to be his special family. God is forming a new universal family to embrace all peoples on earth.

Other Biblical Images of the Church:
- As a plant or plantation (Luke 13:18-19, Matthew 9:37-38, Colossians 1:20-23).
- As flock (Psalm 23, Jeremiah 13:17, Micah 2:12, John 10:1-21).
- As a holy nation (Exodus 19:5-6, 1 Peter 2:9-10, Revelation 5: 11-14, Philippians 2:10-11).
- As ambassadors of Christ (2 Corinthians 5:19-20, 1 Corintios7: 11).
- As a bride or wife (Isaiah 62:5, Hosea 2:19, Matthew 9:15, 25:1-13, Ephesians 5: 25-32, Revelation 19:7-8 and others).

with these truths. In the family of God, all strive to understand each other, and love and support each other. This is the way families stay united and strong. The same sins of selfishness that destroy the human family are equally damaging to the family of faith (Ephesians 5:1 - 6:9).

Characteristics of the Christian Church

In this section, we will study the four characteristics of a Christian church.

Dr. Orton Wiley lists four main features of the Christian church that our denomination teaches and reflects around the world:

1. The Christian church is one, yet diverse in the Spirit and does not seek uniformity.

2. It is holy because it is separated from the world to be dedicated to God, and this holiness is expressed in a clean, pure life with total devotion of its members.

3. It is universal or catholic because it speaks of a universal Christian faith and includes all Christians worldwide from all Christian churches in the world, both those living and those who have died in ages past, including those Christians on earth who fight against evil and those Christians who died and are in the presence of God.

4. It is apostolic, confessional, and is built on the foundation of the apostles and prophets (Ephesians 2:20) as recorded in the Holy Scriptures. The Church confesses Jesus Christ as Lord and Savior (Romans 10:10).

What are the four main features of the Christian church?

The Ministry of the Christian Church

Now we will study the ministry of the church.

Since the Holy Spirit gives different gifts to all Christians to carry out the mission of the church — both within the Body of Christ to build it, and outside of it to reach the lost — there are a variety of service areas.

The church recognizes the special calling that God makes to some people (to men and women regardless of age, nationality, culture, sex or race) to devote all their time to care for and the teach the church (pastors), to leave their culture to reach other cultures (missionaries), or to proclaim the gospel everywhere (evangelists), among others. Another aspect of the ministry of the Christian church is the enjoyment taken in worshipping our God together and in celebrating the means of grace. Also, the Church of the Nazarene takes a special interest in those answering the call of God in their lives and encourages all those who wish to serve God and the church with their gifts.

Finally, the Christian Church exists to continue the mission of Jesus Christ on this earth. No one can destroy it because its founder is alive and He sustains it. The Church will remain the outstretched arm of God in this world to the extent that Christians are committed to Jesus Christ, full of devotion and willing to participate with their service.

What Did We Learn?

The Church of the Nazarene is a Christian church. The Christian Church is one, holy, universal, apostolic and confessional.

The Church of the Nazarene continues the mission of Christ on earth.

You cannot live a Christian life outside the community of believers because that is where growth happens as we encourage each other, work together and express God's love in relationships with others.

Lesson 2 - Our Origin

Activities

Time 20'

INSTRUCTIONS:

1. Write a definition of church in your own words.
   _____
   _____
   _____

2. How can your local church be the Body of Christ? Give examples.
   _____
   _____
   _____

3. Some Christians find it hard to remain in a local church and often change churches. Mention some reasons why people change churches.
   _____
   _____
   _____

4. In groups of 3 people, evaluate the validity of those reasons. Which reasons are valid, which ones are not, and why?
   _____
   _____
   _____

5. In the same groups, list the benefits or advantages of staying in a church. What are the benefits to your life, family and your spiritual growth?
   _____
   _____
   _____

6. How can we help people make the decision to stay, participate and engage with the ministry of our local church?
   _____
   _____
   _____

Lesson 3

OUR FOUNDER

Objectives

- To know the founder of the Church of the Nazarene.
- To learn from his experiences, challenges and convictions.

Main Ideas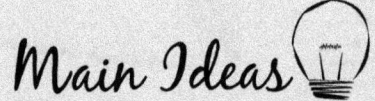

- Phineas F. Bresee lived a consecrated and dedicated life to the ministry.
- Bresee was a person with vision and passion for teaching others to live in holiness.

Introduction

As Nazarenes, it is important to know about the life of Phineas F. Bresee to better appreciate and understand the life and leadership of our founder. In doing so, we identify with his struggles, concerns, worries, accomplishments, convictions, joys, thoughts, vision and sense of mission. Knowing our roots helps us to continue contributing to the formation of the Church of the Nazarene in the present and in the future.

Childhood, Family and Education

Vision: A mental image of what you want in the future.

In this section we learn about the childhood of Dr. Bresee.

Phineas Franklin Bresee was born on December 31, 1838 in the town of Franklin, New York in the eastern United States where he attended primary and secondary school. Phineas was the second of three children in the family.

His parents were Phillip Phineas Bresee, farmer and merchant, and Susan Brown Bresee. His ancestors had fled from France to America to escape religious persecution. His family gathered first with the Dutch Reformed Church, and after learning the teachings of Methodism, remained with that church.

After a while, the family moved to Iowa (Midwest, United States of America). Years later when Phineas married, he brought his parents to live with his family which by this time included seven children (four boys and three girls).

Personality and Character

Now we are going to learn about the person of Rev. Bresee.

Phineas F. Bresee accepted Jesus as his personal Savior at the age of 16 (February 1854) at a Methodist altar, and the following year he was called to the ministry.

Bresee was a young man who took on challenges, faced opposition and worked hard to overcome obstacles because he sincerely believed that God was with him to help prosper his work.

Bresee was sensitive to the needs of others, opposed to social marginalization and participated in campaigns against alcohol. He visited the sick and needy and brought them money and food. He had a passion for evangelizing the poor and extended the ministry of Biblical holiness to everyone.

Above all, Bresee was a young man with a vision. Each church he pastored was a center of revival that clearly preached the gospel and the doctrine of holiness, and this same revival was strongly supported by his actions.

Revival: A time of spiritual awakening that the Holy Spirit brings to the church. It is characterized by a deep desire in believers to live holy lives and to engage in evangelism, teaching and service ministries, resulting in many people repenting and giving their lives to the Lord.

Ministry in Iowa

Now we will learn about his first years in the ministry.

The Methodist Church assigned Phineas Bresee as an assistant pastor to Rev. A.C. Barnhart for one year. A year later in 1858, Bresee was assigned to the area of Pella, Iowa and was given a group of churches to pastor there.

In 1859, Bresee was granted license as a full-time pastor. In 1860, at age 22, he was ordained as a pastor and returned to New York to marry his girlfriend, Mary Hebbard. She was the daughter of Horace Hebbard, a longtime Methodist leader, whose family lived near his childhood home.

During those years, slavery was in effect for the African-Americans and since Bresee did not agree with slavery, he requested a transfer from Pella to another area. He was then assigned to Galesburg, Iowa, which was a very difficult area. Although Bresee was frustrated and bitter with the place, he took it as a challenge to his ministry and asked for guidance and help from God.

After a year, Bresee received 140 new members. With the income they received, the church bought a comfortable parsonage, two horses and a carriage for the pastor. His ministry was bearing much fruit. The church leaders saw this, and he was assigned as pastor of the church at the Methodist University called "Matthew Simpson" in the Iowan capital of Des Moines. He was challenged to design and implement a plan to save the college from financial ruin, which he did after much work and sacrifice.

From then on, Bresee continued to develop as a leader: he acquired much experience in administration and was directly involved in the social problems of his community; he participated in the holiness movement; he demonstrated extraordinary qualities, gifts and talents that he used to preach, teach and promote the doctrine of holiness.

Doctrine: refers to all the beliefs of Christianity (Acts 2:42)

Doctrine of Holiness: The study of the Biblical teachings regarding the purity of heart wrought by the Holy Spirit, resulting in a life devoted to loving God and neighbor with the whole heart (1 Thessalonians 4:3-7).

Lesson 3 - Our Founder

Entire Sanctification: Grace received from God when a believer receives by faith the fullness of the Holy Spirit, which enables him or her to live a life of purity. The will of God is that all his children are wholly sanctified or "saints." The Holy Spirit fills the Christian when he/she understands the need to hand over control of his/her life to the Lordship of Christ, and renounces living that is focused on his/her own will. This is distinguished from the initial sanctification that occurs when the person accepts Christ as their personal Savior (2 Thessalonians 2:13). It is the distinctive doctrine of Arminian-Wesleyan Churches.

> *The theme of holiness was central to the ministry of Bresee.*

At 28 years of age, Bresee experienced entire sanctification after a long search for answers to his questions and doubts about the Christian faith and how he should live. This event took place in one of the prayer meetings of his local church where he was pastor in Chariton, Iowa. One snowy, winter night, after preaching a strong evangelistic message that did not seem to persuade anyone else, Bresee was the only one who knelt before the altar. In front of his congregation, Bresee prayed and received the blessing, which he later called his "baptism with the Holy Spirit" (Bangs, Phineas F. Bresee pp.71-73). He admitted much later that he had not fully realized what occurred, but he was sure that the experience that he had been looking for to satisfy him was received that night.

Ministry in California

In this section we will learn about his ministry in California.

In 1883, Bresee moved his large family to Southern California. The first Sunday after arrival, Pastor E.N. Chase asked Bresee to preach in his church, which was the First Methodist Episcopal Church of Fort Street. This was the central Methodist Church, considered the largest, strongest, oldest and the mother church of all the other Methodist congregations in California.

Phineas Bresee was 45 years old when he was introduced to a new group of Methodist clergy from California at the annual meeting of the Conference, which was held the following week after his arrival. He was given several responsibilities in addition to being assigned as pastor of the First Methodist Church, all of which surprised him.

The population of the city of Los Angeles was growing rapidly, causing many challenges in the city's development (poverty, alcoholism, addiction, hopelessness). Immigrants were coming from Japan and China as cheap labor, adding to the population of Latinos and Americans. Bresee considered these changes in the city and the growing ethnic diversity of the population as opportunities for the church.

After serving three years as pastor at the First Church of Fort Street, he was assigned to pastor the First Methodist Episcopal Church in Pasadena, where he remained for four years. It started with an evangelistic campaign and meetings in the street with construction workers. People turned to Christ and the church grew. In June of 1884, the Simpson Centennial University in Iowa awarded Phineas Bresee the honorary degree of Doctorate of Divinity.

The theme of holiness was central to the ministry of Bresee at the First Methodist Church of Fort Street, but was increasingly emphasized in his ministry in Pasadena. His goal was to "make a fire that reached the sky" and turn the area into a center for evangelism and teaching of Methodist holiness in California. Beginning in 1890, Bresee made the doctrine of holiness the ultimate goal of all his preaching, and this led to many holiness revivals, organized meetings and other activities to promote the doctrine not only in California, but as far away as Illinois.

However, Bresee began to face opposition for promoting the teaching and preaching of holiness, and for his opposition to the sale of liquor. For this reason, Bresee did not return to pastor the church in Pasadena. Then he accepted the invitation of the Asbury Methodist Episcopal Church to be their pastor. He served there for one year (1890-1891). Immediately, Bresee organized holiness revivals with well-known evangelists of that time. Many people were converted and many others were sanctified under the preaching of these servants of God.

Bresee continued identifying more and more with the holiness movement and attended camp meetings in different parts of the country. At the Methodist District Conference meetings, he was assigned to be the elder to chair the meetings of the District of Los Angeles, which had 38 churches. He was elected as deputy minister for the General Conference and a member of various committees. This meant he could no longer continue as pastor at Asbury.

In 1892, Bresee was appointed as pastor of the Simpson Methodist Episcopal Tabernacle in Los Angeles. This church had a huge and beautiful building but was in debt. The poor financial situation of the church was a reflection of the economic situation facing the country as it fell into a deep economic crisis. After many efforts to save the church, Bresee recommended closure. Finally, the building was sold to pay the debt.

In 1893, Bresee was assigned as pastor of the Methodist Episcopal Church in Boyle Heights in the east side of Los Angeles. There he began a series of campaigns and evangelistic holiness activities to bring people to Christ and more Christians to sanctification.

Legacy:
We are heirs to the extraordinary heritage of the life of Phineas F. Bresee, of the founders of the early Nazarenes and of the history of our denomination. This legacy is described in many books describing the lives of these pioneers, their ministries, their challenges and struggles, their positions on various theological issues and their thoughts and philosophies about the ministry. This legacy also includes their writings and sermons that are an inspiration to the church and that nurture the identity of the Nazarenes today.

The Beginnings of the Church of the Nazarene

In this section we will learn about the events that led to the origin of our denomination.

In early 1894, Theodore P. Ferguson (a traveling evangelist) and his wife Manie Payne from the Newton Mission (an independent, holiness mission, formerly Methodist) in San Francisco, sought help from Phineas Bresee to plan and open an interdenominational rescue mission. They got money to buy property in downtown Los Angeles and to start the program. At first, Bresee was not interested, but then agreed to help them carry out this project.

The Peniel Mission was a meeting place for the laity of the holiness movement from all parts of the United States and for the poor of the city. Those who supervised the work included Ferguson, Bresee, and George B.

Laity: Every believer of a local church, excluding the ministers (licensed or ordained).

Lesson 3 - Our Founder

Studd. Bresee agreed to be the pastor, preaching on Sunday mornings and editing the newsletter "The Herald of Peniel." J. P. Widney, a friend of Bresee, agreed to preach on Sunday nights and help with medical consultations for the poor.

At the annual meeting of the Methodist Conference, Bresee asked the district leader to ask permission from the bishop to grant him the regular assignment as the pastor of the Peniel Mission. This mission was not a ministry of the Methodist Church, so the request was denied. When this was not approved, Bresee asked for a special status which in those days was called "license" status, but the situation did not apply under the policies of the Methodist Church. Upon finding himself unable to help with the church or the work he had been doing without going against the denomination, he began to pray to make a decision about what to do.

Bresee had felt a burden for working with the poor and was convinced that God had called him to the work, so he requested and received from the Methodist Church special elder status or local preacher status. This allowed him to be free of a responsibility to pastor a church to engage in mission work with Widney and the mission's founders, Theodore P. and his wife Manie Ferguson. In May 1895, conflicts began between the organizers of the Peniel Mission and Bresee due to their different perspectives on various issues and the differences in doctrinal emphasis on holiness. So, taking advantage of the fact that Bresee was preaching at the Association of Holiness camp meetings out of town and Widney had gone to study for one year to the East Coast, the organizers notified them both that they were terminating their relationship with the mission.

Soon after, the group of Methodist laypersons who had followed Bresee to the Peniel Mission took the initiative to rent a small place and asked Bresee and Widney be the leaders of the new work. Bresee, 58 years old, was the pastor of this group who began to gather in a large room called Red Men's Hall on October 6, 1895. Both Bresee and Widney wanted to organize a new church where the rich and the poor were welcome, and where they would allow people that did not belong to a church to be part of a mission that could be a spiritual home for them.

Bresee's friends, their families and other Methodist leaders joined him in the work. The group grew from eighty to over one hundred people. On Sunday October 20th the church was formally organized with the name Church of the Nazarene. Widney chose the nickname "The Nazarene" as a name that symbolized the work that Jesus did among the poor. Christ's contemporaries used the term in a derogatory sense because Nazareth was a city with a bad reputation. Widney preached his message based on the Gospel of Matthew 4:19 where Jesus invited Peter to follow Him and live a life of service. He further explained that this new church was designed to reach the poor for Christ.

The organization began enrolling members, and at the end of the service the people were asked to promise to God and to each other, their faithfulness

Bresee's Ministerial Experience
Evangelist, preacher, pastor, district superintendent, editor, director, delegate, local missionary, college president, businessman, construction foreman, organizer, administrator and general superintendent. All these experiences and responsibilities helped Bresee in the development of his spiritual character, his gifts, talents and skills, and above all, leadership and ministry, which later would bring him to lead a denomination.

in the establishment and development of the church, knowing that its purpose was to preach holiness and carry the message of salvation to the poor.

On Wednesday, October 30, the new church leaders met to give form to the organization, or in other words, to define the Church of the Nazarene which included the following: adopt the Articles of Faith (7) which joined them to their Methodist and Anglican roots, establish policies, elect officers, and incorporate the church under the laws of the State of California. They also defined an organizational structure that was similar to that of the Methodist churches with some variations (pastoral bodies, stewards, local board, Sunday School superintendent, district assemblies, deacons, clergy, general superintendents, pastors, local church board presidents, membership regulations, etc.). The distinction between Methodism of that day and the Church of the Nazarene was that the new church gave equal rights to men and women to serve in any position of the church, including as elders.

Bresee and Widney were appointed as pastors of the first congregation and as the denomination's General Superintendents to supervise and direct the work. The young church, enthusiastic and growing, continued to add members; they reached 300 people and eight years later reached 1,500 people. They also produced a number of daughter churches in different parts of California and outside the state as well.

Bresee continued as full-time pastor, but he was also editor of a newsletter of the church and president of a university. As they celebrated the first general assembly in Chicago, Illinois, the Church of the Nazarene had fifty congregations. It was at this point that the idea of the Church of the Nazarene uniting with other holiness groups that existed in the east and south of the country became clearer.

Bresee served as General Superintendent of the Church of the Nazarene until his death on November 13, 1915, at 77 years of age. In that same year, not long before he died, the fourth General Assembly was held in Kansas City and the leaders took advantage of the opportunity to pay a living tribute to their founding leader in a special ceremony where the other founders were present as well as the delegates.

Key Influences in the Life of Bresee
- The itinerant preachers of New York.
- The Methodist societies of West Davenport where he grew in discipleship. Bishop Matthew Simpson was one of his heroes in ministry.
- The laity of the First Methodist Church of Fort Street, Los Angeles, who professed holiness. Leslie F. Gay in whose home they celebrated the holiness services.
- The great holiness evangelists of the time: RW Farmsworth, William McDonald, George D. Watson, T.E. Robinson, A.J. Bell and J.A. Wood.

What Did We Learn?

Phineas F. Bresee was a simple, passionate, sensitive, persistent and committed person with a strong vision.
Bresee was a spiritual and charismatic leader with deep convictions.
Bresee received valuable influences in his life for his spiritual growth, ministry and leadership.

Activities

Time 20'

INSTRUCTIONS:

1. What most impacted you about the life of Phineas F. Bresee?
   _____
   _____
   _____

2. Make a poster to display in your local church with information about the life of Phineas F. Bresse. You may search on the Internet or in denominational literature for more information.
   _____
   _____
   _____

3. What is your opinion on Bresee's fight against poverty, alcoholism, and slavery? What are the issues that the church should deal with in your community today?
   _____
   _____
   _____

4. What are your thoughts on Bresee's passion for preaching and teaching the doctrine of holiness?
   _____
   _____
   _____

5. Do you think that the contemporary church needs leadership with the same passion that Bresee had? Why?
   _____
   _____
   _____

6. Analyzing influences on Breese's life, how can we today form leaders who are passionate about teaching others to live in holiness?
   _____
   _____
   _____

Lesson 4

OUR HISTORY

Objectives

- To trace the origins of the denomination.
- To highlight important aspects of the history.
- To value the characteristics and contributions of its founders.

Main Ideas

- The Church of the Nazarene was strengthened by bringing together many of the Holiness churches in the eastern and southern United States.
- The rapid growth was due to the fact that its members lived and taught the doctrine of holiness, radically influencing their community and their nation.

Introduction

The history of the Church of the Nazarene is one of the components of our identity that unites all Nazarenes around the world because it is an exciting story of God's work in the life of a nation and in the hearts of the leaders and the first Nazarenes in the denomination.

Denomination: A group of local churches in different places that share similar beliefs, historical roots, purposes and values.

The Nazarene lineage came about through the English Reformation and the international spread of Methodism and the Wesleyan Holiness movement in the United States of America. The Church of the Nazarene emerged as a union of various Wesleyan Holiness denominations, primarily in the United States. Later, other holiness groups from several world countries joined the denomination.

What Are the Historical Foundations of the Church of the Nazarene?

In this section we will study the roots of our church.

In the *Historical Statement of the Manual of the Church of the Nazarene*, it states that the church sees itself as an integral part of the universal Church.

The history of the Church of the Nazarene begins with the story of the people of God as recorded in the Old and New Testaments and continues through the centuries in the history of the Christian believers in all parts of the world.

The Church of the Nazarene accepts the great ecumenical creeds of the first five centuries of Christian history as expressions of faith and as fundamental to its identity.

The Church of the Nazarene believes that it has a special mission that is God-given.

The Church of the Nazarene is a Protestant church in the sense that it accepts the principles of the Reformation of the sixteenth century.

The Church of the Nazarene has its heritage in the Wesleyan revival of the seventeenth century in England led by John and Charles Wesley whose central focus was the doctrine of Christian perfection.

The Church of the Nazarene is a holiness church because it grew out of the holiness movement in the United States in the nineteenth century through the union of several independent holiness groups.

What Are the Origins of the Church of the Nazarene?

Now we will study the beginnings of the denomination.

The founder of the church was Rev. Phineas F. Bresee, a Methodist minister who served as pastor, evangelist and District Superintendent of the Methodist Episcopal Church for 37 years. An admirable leader, with deep convictions that were evident in his ministerial work, he believed in and promoted the Biblical doctrine of entire sanctification. However, he received opposition to the proclamation of the holiness message and to his given ministry, even by his own colleagues.

"And he went and lived in a town called Nazareth. So was fulfilled what was said through the prophets, that he would be called a Nazarene."
Matthew 2:23 NIV

Bresee noted that the church grew rapidly with the help of good leaders and friends, so Bresee, along with Dr. Joseph P. Widney, a doctor and Methodist layperson, decided to organize the church. (They had worked together before in a rescue mission to help the poor, the immigrants, and the factory and construction workers in the city of Penial, Los Angeles, California, USA). The Church of the Nazarene was organized in October of 1895 with more than 100 people. They adopted a declaration of faith and agreed to some simple general rules that served to guide the practice of the Christian life.

In the following years, the local congregation not only grew in number, but geographically as well. The church opened works in neighboring areas and even in other nearby states. Very soon they were not only in California and the surrounding area, but were reaching all the way to Illinois. The teachings of holiness were spread in strategic locations throughout the country, becoming centers of revival for the nation.

"We have found this man to be a troublemaker, stirring up riots among the Jews all over the world. He is a ringleader of the Nazarene sect."
Acts 24:5 NIV

Over the years the church flourished and there were many holiness preachers and evangelists who traveled the country teaching, preaching and promoting the doctrine of holiness. The motto of the church was *"Holiness unto the Lord."*

Lesson 4 - Our History

How Did the Church of the Nazarene Get Its Name?

In this section we will learn about the name of the denomination.

It was Dr. Widney who suggested the name Church of the Nazarene for the new denomination because they wanted to identify with the ministry of Jesus and also symbolize the work they had been doing with the poor.

Dr. Widney based the name on the passage from Matthew 2:23 where it says that Jesus moved to Nazareth to fulfill what the prophets had spoken, that he would be called "the Nazarene." In Acts 24:5 it mentions that the followers of Jesus were called Nazarenes or were part of the sect of the Nazarenes.

What Distinguished the Church of the Nazarene at the Beginning?

How did the first Nazarenes teach and preach holiness?

Now we will study 10 characteristics of the first Nazarenes.

The Church of the Nazarene distinguished itself from other holiness groups by the following:

1. Women and men worked together in the ministry of the church serving in all areas and ministerial positions without discrimination.
2. There was a commitment and sensitivity to the needs of the poor and broken.
3. The members had a vision of a far-reaching ministry, varied and international. It was not confined to one area of ministry, neither was the work confined to the local church, urban ministry or a single country.
4. The church emphasized education as an important and key part of a Wesleyan heritage church and a holiness church. It promoted the teaching of Christian values for children, youth and adults, as well as training and preparation for professional careers and theological studies.
5. The heart and reason for existing was the doctrine of entire sanctification. This was the church's motivation in its mission.
6. There was a continuous conversion of sinners and sanctification of believers.
7. It was a church made up of people who continually interceded in prayer for one another.
8. It was a church that showed joy in their worship and praise to the Lord.

General Superintendent
The Church of the Nazarene has a General Superintendent for each of the regions of the world in which the church is geographically divided for administrative purposes. These are elected in the general assembly held every four years with delegates from all districts. The general superintendents are responsible for ensuring the unity of the church and the permanence of it in the Biblical doctrine. They attend to administrative matters in their jurisdiction, direct district assemblies and grant ministerial ordination to clergy and deacons.

9. They had conviction and security in their experience of holiness.
10. They taught and preached holiness continually and in many creative ways.

These features increasingly attracted many people, even members of other denominations. The church grew rapidly and this was due to several factors: the church contributed to the spiritual renewal of Christianity, the church emphasized the teaching and experience of the Biblical doctrine of sanctification, the members gave evidence of this holy life and they radically influenced their community and their nation. The church's fame became so widespread that the Church of the Nazarene was included in the list of sights to visit in Los Angeles. These factors from past years remain a goal for the church today.

How Did the Holiness Groups Unite with the Nazarene Church?

In this section we will study the merger that created the denomination.

In several places in the United States, independent holiness churches, urban missions, rescue missions, missionary societies, and evangelistic associations were developing. It was common for churches to come together to strengthen each other. Many independent churches came together and formed associations bearing the same name. On the east side of the country there were three different groups: the Central Evangelical Holiness Association, the Association of Pentecostal Churches North America and three independent holiness churches. On the south side of the country there were two groups: the Holiness Christian Church and the Methodist Association of Laity. On the west side of the country were the Church of the Nazarene and the First Pentecostal Mission.

After a series of visits, talks, meetings and correspondence about beliefs, forms of government, issues of leadership and ministries, mission and vision, assets and property, among others, these groups decided to merge as a large holiness body.

In the week of October 10-18, 1907, the Association of Pentecostal Churches of America united with the Church of the Nazarene and elected two General Superintendents, one from each group (Bresee and Reynolds). They shared the name: The Pentecostal Church of the Nazarene.

In September of the following year, another holiness church joined the new denomination, and then on October 8, 1908, the groups from the east, west, and south merged in Pilot Point, Texas. Later on, the General Assembly of 1923 chose the year 1908 as the official year to celebrate the anniversary of the denomination.

Lesson 4 - Our History

General Superintendents of the Church of the Nazarene
- Phineas F. Bresee (1895-1915)
- Hiram F. Reynolds (1907-1932)
- E.P. Ellyson (1980 - 1911)
- E.F. Walker (1911 - 1918)
- W.C. Wilson (1915)
- J.W. Goodwin (1916-1940)
- R.T. William (1916-1946)
- J.B. Chapman (1928 - 1947)
- J.G. Morrison (1936-1939)
- H.V. Miller (1940-1948)
- Orval J. Nease (1940-1944)
- Hardy C. Powers (1944-1968)
- G.B. Williamson (1946-1968)
- Samuel Young (1948-1972)
- D.I. Vanderpool (1949-1964)
- Hugh C. Benner (1952-1968)
- V.H. Lewis (1960-1985)
- George Coulter (1964-1980)
- Edward G. Lawlor (1968-1976)
- Eugene L. Stowe (1968-1993)
- Orville W. Jenkins (1968-1985)
- Charles H. Strickland (1972-1988)
- William M. Greathouse (1976-1989)
- Jerald D. Johnson (1980-1997)
- John A. Knight (1985-2001)
- William J. Prince (1989-2001)
- Donald D. Owens (1989-1997)
- James H. Diehl (1993-2009)
- Paul G. Cunningham (1993-2009)
- Jerry D. Porter (1997)
- Jim L. Bond (1997-2005)
- W. Talmadge Johnson (2001-2005)
- Jesse C. Middendorf (2001)
- Nina G. Gunter (2005-2009)
- J.K. Warrick (2005)
- Eugenio Duarte (2009)
- David W. Graves (2009)
- Stanley A. Toler (2009)

Important Leaders:

- George Sharpe, a pioneer of the movement of church holiness in Great Britain, especially in Scotland, who later joined the denomination, contributed with his fruitful ministry to the preaching of holiness.

- James O. McClurkan, founder of a leading association of holiness in Tennessee who joined the denomination, was known for his missionary zeal and practical theology. He emphasized education and missions abroad.

- C.B. Jernigan, a pioneer and great holiness preacher, helped organize independent bands of holiness in an association of churches in the southern United States who later joined the denomination.

- J.G. Morrison, leader active in the Holiness movement, organized the Association of Lay Holiness in the northwestern United States, formed by a large group of evangelists and Christian workers who joined the denomination.

- C.W. Ruth, evangelist of the National Holiness Association and leader in the eastern United States, who proposed to the Association of Pentecostal Churches of America that they merge with the denomination.

In 1915, other holiness groups in the United States and Scotland joined the denomination.

The General Assembly of 1919, in response to the request of the assemblies of thirty-five districts, removed the word "Pentecostal" in the name of the denomination and took the original name of Church of the Nazarene. The former name was causing confusion about the doctrinal position of the church, and the church did not want to be identified with the modern Pentecostal movement that emphasized the gift of tongues as evidence of the baptism of the Holy Spirit.

In 1922, 1952, 1955, 1958 and 1988 several holiness groups from the United States, Canada, England, Nigeria and South Africa joined the international denomination with churches in the Caribbean, Central America, South America, Asia, Africa and Cape Verde.

In the foundational period of 1911, the Nazarene Publishing House was created. In 1912 the denominational magazine "The Herald of Holiness" was published. Also during this time mission work was established in different countries, and several universities were developed to educate Christian ministers and lay leaders.

From 1915 to 1945, the church formed the foreign missionary society, created the general board and established the Sunday School department. Later in the period from 1946 to 1970, the missionary work spread to other nations of the world, the Nazarene Theological Seminary was founded (1945), radio broadcasts in English, Spanish and other languages began and youth mission groups also started.

From 1971 onwards, the church emphasized and worked on the international nature of the denomination, as well as strengthened compassionate ministries and other programs.

In the year 2000 and the decades leading up to it, the denomination continued to renew and update itself. New and innovative ministries started at all levels (local, district, regional, and general church) to work with children, youth and adults. In addition to developing new service areas for lay people, the church designed new strategies for evangelism and church growth and established new and practical theological education programs to prepare and train more ministers.

The church also used new media and computer technology to broadcast programs, videos, promotions, communications, publications and other materials. It created new educational programs for discipleship and spiritual formation of members. Many new books were written and published in different areas, the number of mission/intercultural trips increased both inside and outside of each country, and the number of international conferences to promote the doctrine of holiness increased.

The church has had an international dimension from the beginning; therefore, it continues to be a global denomination growing around the world with a membership of over 1.2 million people.

Founding Leaders of the Denomination

Phineas F. Bresee, minister, evangelist, founder of the denomination, the first General Superintendent, who developed the form of church government.

Hiram F. Reynolds, minister, second General Superintendent, nurtured the identity as a church committed to international missions.

Edgar P. Ellyson, minister, theologian, third General Superintendent, contributed in the area of education for the denomination, the preparation of leaders and Sunday school.

Roy T. Williams, minister, General Superintendent, shared his experience as pastor and evangelist and his knowledge as a professor of theology and Bible.

James B. Chapman, minister, General Superintendent, gave the church a rich legacy of holiness literature and holiness preaching.

Sister Denominations of the Church of the Nazarene

The sister denominations are those which, while maintaining a separate organization, share similar doctrines with the Church of the Nazarene.

The Wesleyan holiness denominations that are distinguished by their common belief in the doctrine of entire sanctification and that arose within the Wesleyan tradition are as follows:

The Free Methodist Church, The Wesleyan Church and the Salvation Army.

The additional denominations listed below did not come out of the Wesleyan tradition, but they adopted the doctrine of entire sanctification as an article of faith and therefore are considered Holiness churches.

The Church of God (Anderson, Indiana), Holiness Church of God, Holiness Church of Christ, Missionary Bible Church, the Brethren in Christ, Friends Church and Christian Missionary Alliance.

Other Prominent Leaders:

-William Howard Hoople, one of the twelve founders of the denomination, who founded the Church of Utica Avenue and other holiness churches in New York.

-MaryLee Cagle, holiness preacher, whose ordination opened the way for many women in the Holiness movement who were called by God to public ministry. She was a great evangelist, church planter and pastor.

-Susan Fitkin, the first president of the Missionary Society and often called the "mother of missions." She promoted, began and established the mission movement in the denomination. She sent out more than 1700 missionaries during her ministry.

-Reuben (Bud) Robinson, a strong, southern leader who evangelized with great passion to hundreds of people during his ministry.

-H.O. Wiley, a minister, educator, theologian and writer, who contributed through his commitment to education as an integral part of holiness.

What Did We Learn?

The history of the Church of the Nazarene is an exciting story of God's work in a nation and in the hearts of the people.

The Church of the Nazarene is the result of a holiness revival that found expression in unity.

To understand the history of the Church of the Nazarene, one has to understand the founders and the development of the denomination.

Lesson 4 - Our History

Activities

Time 20'

INSTRUCTIONS:

1. Write the biography of a leader of the Church of the Nazarene, whether a founder of the denomination (United States) or a founder of the work in your country (missionary or national leader), whose life has inspired you. Then do a presentation to the group or local church or send it to your contacts via the Internet.

2. Research by interviewing older members of your local church to find some interesting facts or anecdotes of the founders and history of your location.

3. What was the most important thing that you learned in this lesson?

Lesson 5

OUR BELIEFS

Objectives

- To know our basic beliefs.
- To identify key aspects of our theological identity.
- To appreciate the doctrine of entire sanctification.

Main Ideas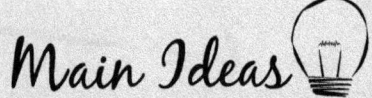

- The Church of the Nazarene shares the creeds of the Christian churches and the principles of the Reformation movement.
- The theological tradition of the Church of the Nazarene is Wesleyan-Armenian.
- Sanctification is God's work to clean the believer's heart so that it is pure and full of God's love.

The basic doctrines of Christianity are expressed in the Apostles' Creed:
I believe in God the Father Almighty, maker of heaven and earth;
And in Jesus Christ his only Son our Lord: who was conceived by the Holy Spirit, born of the Virgin Mary, suffered under Pontius Pilate, was crucified, dead, and buried;
the third day he rose from the dead; he ascended into heaven,
and sitteth at the right hand of God the Father Almighty; from thence he shall come to judge the quick and the dead.
I believe in the Holy Spirit, the holy catholic church,
the communion of saints, the forgiveness of sins,
the resurrection of the body, and the life everlasting. Amen.

catholic: When it is not capitalized, it refers to the universal Church, the body of Christ and is accepted by Protestants and Roman Catholics.

Introduction

The Church of the Nazarene is a Christian church that is founded on the principles and values of the Bible. It is also a church with a passion to teach, preach and live the Biblical doctrine of holiness. This makes a difference in how Nazarenes think and live in the world.

What Do Nazarenes Believe?

In this section we will learn about the basic beliefs of Nazarenes.

We believe we are a part of the universal Church of Jesus Christ and that we share with other Christian communities the same Lord, the same faith and the same baptism.

We believe the Old and New Testament reveal God's will for people concerning sin, salvation and new life in Christ.

We believe in the basic doctrines of Christianity formed in the great ecumenical creeds of the early centuries of the Christian Church.

We believe and affirm that salvation is by grace through faith, that Scripture is the final authority for faith and practice of Christian life and we believe in the priesthood of all believers.

We believe that Christians are justified and sanctified through faith.

We believe that Jesus Christ's sanctifying grace is received in the new birth (regeneration) when the Holy Spirit implants new spiritual life in the believer and that this sanctifying grace increases as we live in the Spirit.

We believe and affirm that entire sanctification is a gracious provision for all believers where the heart is cleansed of all sin and filled with love for God and others.

School of Leadership - The DNA of the Nazarenes

What Was Included in the Original Nazarene Articles of Faith?

In this section we will learn about our Articles of Faith.

In October 1895, Bresse and the leaders adopted a short creed that emphasized the essential aspects of salvation. Now called the Articles of Faith, it is located in Part II of the Constitution of the Church in the Manual of the Church of the Nazarene. These are the original statements of faith from the 1895 Manual.

We believe:

1. In one God, the Father, Son, and Holy Spirit.
2. That the Scriptures of the Old and New Testaments are fully inspired and contain all truth necessary for faith and Christian life.
3. That man is born with a fallen nature and is therefore continually inclined to evil.
4. The person who does not repent of their sins is without hope and is eternally lost.
5. That the atonement of Jesus Christ is for all mankind and whosoever repents and believes in the Lord Jesus Christ is justified and regenerated and saved from the dominion of sin.
6. That believers are to be sanctified completely, subsequent to regeneration through faith in Jesus Christ.
7. That the Holy Spirit testifies to the new believer in regeneration and entire sanctification.
8. That our Lord will return, the dead will be resurrected, the final judgment will occur to reward believers and punish those who have rejected Jesus Christ.

What Are the Nazarene Articles of Faith?

Now we will study the current Articles of Faith.

The original statement of faith was reformulated and extended and is expressed in fourteen points called "doctrinal statements" that appeared in the 1908 Manual of the Pentecostal Church of the Nazarene. Years later, at different times, the order was varied and doctrinal statements were added concerning the topic of divine healing (although it was present before but under the Special Advice section) and the church. These are the doctrinal statements set forth in the following 16 articles of faith:

I. The Triune God
II. Jesus Christ
III. The Holy Spirit

Lesson 5 - Our Beliefs

Principles of the Protestant Reformation:
- The Scriptures are the only source of authority and are sufficient for faith.
- Salvation is by grace through faith alone.
- The priesthood of all believers.
- Jesus Christ alone is the head of the Church.

Atonement: Refers to the death of Christ in place of the sinner, who paid, by His innocent death, the cost of God's justice, which is demanded to erase the stain of sin that separated man from God. It is through Christ's death that God could reconcile the world and through his death the way was opened for union with God for all human beings (2 Corinthians 5:19, Hebrews 2:17).

REGENERATION:
This word it used to describe the work of restoration that the Spirit of God causes in the person who accepts Christ as their personal Savior. Regenerated means made new or born again (John 3:3).

Justified: A person who has just been made or declared righteous by God (Romans 5:1).

Plenary Inspiration of the Scriptures

Inspiration is "that actuating energy of the Holy Spirit, guided by which the human agents chosen by God have officially proclaimed His will by word of mouth, or have committed to writing the several portions of the Bible" (Introduction to Christian Theology, Orton Wiley, p.168). The Church of the Nazarene believes that the entire Bible is the Word of God. Its authors were "inspired" by God, that is to say, they were led by God Himself to provide the human race enough information to live in obedience to the Creator. God has provided a sure guide for anyone who wants to live every day in holiness by following the example of Jesus (Luke 14:44-47), 1 Corinthians 15:3-4, 2 Timothy 3:15-17, 2 Peter 1:20-21).

IV. The Holy Scriptures
V. Sin, Original and Personal
VI. Atonement
VII. Prevenient Grace
VIII. Repentance
IX. Justification, Regeneration and Adoption
X. Christian Holiness and Entire Sanctification
XI. The Church
XII. Baptism
XIII. The Lord's Supper
XIV. Divine Healing
XV. Second Coming of Christ
XVI. Resurrection, Judgment, and Destiny

Our Articles of Faith are a reflection of the 25 Articles of Faith of Methodism and these in turn of the 39 Articles of Anglicanism.

What Is the Nazarene Theological Tradition?

In this section we will learn about our theological heritage.

The theological tradition of the Church of the Nazarene is Wesleyan-Arminian because we believe and affirm the Biblical doctrines taught by John Wesley and James Arminius.

James Arminius (1550-1609) was a Dutch pastor and preacher in the Reformed Church, a theologian, a professor and a doctor of theology. He wrote many theological papers in defense of the faith. He addressed the issues of predestination, the relationship between God and man, the order of the church, the regeneration of man according to Romans chapter 7, baptism, grace and free will.

Arminius taught the doctrine of grace (grace is free for all), the doctrine of free will (where one can choose God to be saved or one can reject His offer of salvation), the doctrine of perseverance of the saints (that saving grace may be lost through severe and persistent sin), the doctrine of justification (salvation is conditioned upon faith and repentance), the doctrine of predestination (Jesus died for all humans), the doctrine of sin, the doctrine of sanctification, the doctrine of the church and the doctrine of the sacraments.

John Wesley (1703-1791) was an Anglican pastor, evangelist, British Christian theologian and founder of Methodism. John and his brother Charles (1707-1788) led the great revival in England. Wesley wrote thousands of books, pamphlets and letters to disseminate his theological thinking.

Wesley taught the doctrine of the means of grace and the sacraments, the doctrine of prevenient grace (that which draws us to salvation), the doctrine of the witness of the Spirit, the doctrine of original sin and personal sin, the doctrine of Scripture, doctrine of Christian perfection, creation doctrine, the doctrine of church and worship, doctrine of God, doctrine of salvation by faith, doctrine of personal security, and the doctrine of the end times or the end of the world.

What Do Nazarenes Believe About Entire Sanctification?

In this section we will learn about our principle doctrine.

Dr. Rob Staples, one of the theologians of the denomination, explains sanctification as the lifelong process of becoming holy as we are called to be, where holiness is made perfect through the fear of God and moving us by means of grace to our destiny. That destiny is defined by the image of God by which humans have been created, but because of sin, that image remained tarnished until the image was revealed to us in Jesus Christ. The Son of God incarnate is the image of the invisible God and was sent to us as the life model to follow. Therefore, our destiny is to be shaped and transformed into the image of Jesus Christ, and that is the essence of sanctification.

Sanctification is both instantaneous and progressive with very definite stages starting with justification (initial sanctification), gradual growth (progressive sanctification) until another moment when the heart is cleansed from all sin and filled with love for God and neighbor (entire sanctification). It is God who does the work of "making us holy" in response to our consecration.

This work of grace of sanctification is obtained in the here and now as part of the believer's life on Earth (in a long or short time period) and continues to grow until the believer enters the presence of God (glorification). The Holy Spirit performs this work of purification that requires faith and not works.

What Do Nazarenes Believe About Christian Perfection?

We will now learn Wesleyan teaching concerning Christian perfection.

Nazarenes understand that the Spirit fills us with perfect love, the same perfect love of God himself. "To be perfect," means to love God with all your heart and with all your soul and with all your strength and your neighbor as yourself, and love even your enemies.

Anglicanism: This refers to the Church of England, which is the official church of the country. Their ministry leaders are bishops, the elders or priests and deacons. The liturgy is based on the Book of Common Prayer. The member churches include the Episcopal Protestant Church.

Initial Sanctification: This refers to the baptism of the Spirit that is received at conversion when the believer is born into a spiritual life. John Wesley called it this according to his understanding of the doctrine of holiness and in order to affirm that the Holy Spirit comes and immediately begins the work in the heart of the person who has received Jesus Christ as their personal Savior.

Lesson 5 - Our Beliefs

> **Progressive sanctification:** This term refers to the believer's growth process in purity due to the internal work of the Holy Spirit transferring to the Christian the character of Christ.

This love is not conditional, but just as the love of God is by grace, this same grace is what allows us to love even those who persecute us or mistreat us. The Scriptures teach that we must be good and fair to everyone (friends and enemies). Therefore, being perfect refers to having maturity of character, and showing love and compassion for all others in all circumstances. In this way, we reflect the character of God and we show our obedience, growing in the image and likeness of Jesus Christ.

Wesley said that if a believer maintains this perfect love in life then that means the believer is exercising the power to not voluntarily sin. Thus, both new believers and mature Christians have the power to not willingly transgress the commandments of God.

With Christian perfection, the issue goes beyond just having the power to not sin, but has to do with the inner being of the person.

In Wesley's doctrine on Christian perfection, he makes it very clear that a Christian is not perfect, nor should expect to be perfect. He says that believers are not perfect in knowledge, they are not free from making errors in the things of life that are not essential to salvation, and they are not free from human limitations (being slow to understand, having incoherent thinking, being confused, etc.). They are not free from temptations, and do not have a static perfection, but a dynamic perfection.

> **Consecration:** The act of dedicating something exclusively to God's service. This can be the life of a person, their time and/or belongings, among other things (Romans 6:13-19, 12:1).

For Wesley, the perfect Christian is one who has a heart filled with love that is patient, gentle, and humble and one who has control of the temper, thoughts, words and actions.

Doctrinal Distinctions of the Church of the Nazarene

In this section we will learn about doctrinal differences between denominations.

There are many Christian traditions that emphasize one aspect of the truth or one way of interpreting a teaching of Scripture. Some teachings in which the Nazarenes differ from other denominations are as follows:

We do not accept the doctrine of unconditional election or predestination from the Calvinist tradition that says that before birth God choose that every human being would either be saved or be lost forever. This doctrine proposes that regardless if a person continues in sin, he or she will be saved because the person has been chosen or "predestined" for it.

We do not accept limited atonement from the fundamentalist beliefs claiming that Christ's sacrifice only benefits a limited number of human beings.

Nor does the Nazarene church accept the emphasis on the gift of tongues as evidence of the fullness of the Holy Spirit, or the use of a prayer language

School of Leadership - The DNA of the Nazarenes

other than one's own language as evidence of a greater degree of spirituality, as some Pentecostal churches affirm.

What Are the Convictions that Began the Church of the Nazarene?

In the last section we will learn about the beliefs that gave birth to the denomination.

1. Nazarenes are committed to being good stewards of the doctrine of the Christian faith received from the Christian Church.
2. Nazarenes know that what unites them with other Christians is more important than what differentiates them.
3. Nazarenes believe strongly that the message of the gospel has the power to transform the lives of everyone who receives it.
4. Nazarenes believe that God has raised up the Church of the Nazarene with a mission to all humanity: to live a life without sin, to witness to and teach others to live a holy life and to practice perfect love following the example of Jesus of Nazareth.
5. Nazarenes believe that the Scriptures are the only source of authority for faith and practice of the Christian life.
6. Nazarenes appreciate, value and respect cultural diversity because they understand that it enriches the church.

What Did We Learn?

Nazarenes teach, preach and live the Biblical doctrine of holiness as a divine work of cleansing sin from the heart, as a response to consecration, where the fullness of God's love allows the person to love fully their neighbor and even their enemies, as part of the transformational process and likeness to Jesus Christ. The Nazarene beliefs are based on scripture and the teachings of John Wesley.

Lesson 5 - Our Beliefs

Activities

Time 20'

INSTRUCTIONS:

1. What is the Biblical doctrine that gave the Church of the Nazarene its identity?
   _____
   _____

2. After reading Romans 12, explain in your own words what complete consecration means.
   _____
   _____

3. What is your personal experience regarding consecration, the fullness of the Spirit and the life of holiness?
   _____
   _____

4. What are the differences between the beliefs of the Nazarene Church in comparison with other Christian theological traditions regarding sanctification?
   _____
   _____

5. Why is the theological tradition of the Nazarenes called Wesleyan-Arminian? Also, mention the names of two major theologians.
   _____
   _____

6. In groups of 3 or 4, mention specific examples of how to express holiness in the everyday life of the believer.
   _____ _____ _____
   _____ _____ _____
   _____ _____ _____

7. End the class with a time of prayer for those who want to be sanctified by the work of the Holy Spirit.

Lesson 6

OUR ORGANIZATION

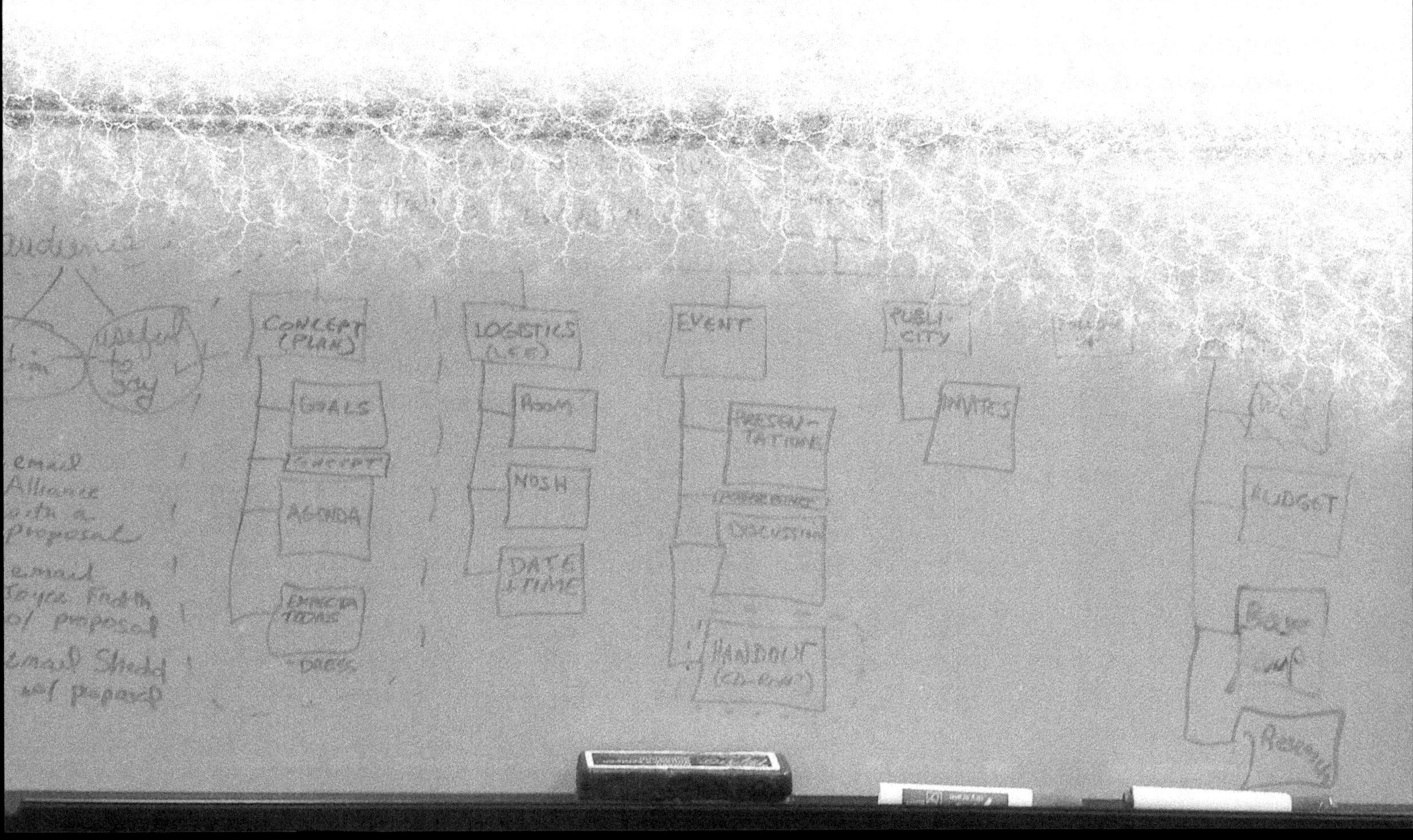

Objectives

- To understand the organizational structure of the denomination.
- To assess how the organization functions to fulfill its mission.

Main Ideas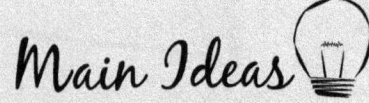

- Understanding our organizational structure helps us to appreciate our denomination.
- Leadership and organization are needed to lead the church in fulfilling its mission in the world.
- Some aspects of our organizational structure are inherited from the Anglican and Methodist heritage.

Introduction

This lesson will examine the organization of the Church of the Nazarene to understand how it functions, its form of government, how leaders are chosen, how decisions are made, and how the Church of the Nazarene develops programs and ministries.

The Manual of the Church of the Nazarene

In this section we will understand why the Manual is necessary.

The Preamble of Part II " Church Constitution" gives reasons as to why we have a manual:
"In order that we may preserve our God-given heritage, the faith once delivered to the saints, especially the doctrine and experience of entire sanctification as a second work of grace, and also that we may cooperate effectually with other branches of the Church of Jesus Christ in advancing God's kingdom, we, the ministers and lay members of the Church of the Nazarene, in accordance with the principles of constitutional legislation established among us, do hereby ordain, adopt, and set forth as the fundamental law or Constitution of the Church of the Nazarene the Articles of Faith, the Covenant of Christian Character, and the Articles of Organization and Government…" (Manual, 2013-2017, Preamble, p. 28).

The Manual of the Church of the Nazarene is a guide that contains, in an orderly and systematic way, information on the history, beliefs, organization, government, objectives, functions, procedures, mission, values, ethical practices and official positions of the denomination. It is an instrument of administrative support for leaders and is efficient for the work of the denomination.

The knowledge and application of the Manual offers several advantages: it presents a global vision of the organization of the denomination; it clearly states the functions of each administrative area, each ministry and each position of service; it facilitates unity in the work in order to fulfill the mission of the Church; and it saves time and effort executing functions. It also provides information about the beliefs and positions of the denomination in important matters, assists in the planning, organizing, coordinating, delegating and evaluating of the work, and serves as a means of integrating the new local churches in different countries around the world, facilitating the incorporation and integration into the denomination.

Every four years the General Assembly revises and updates the Manual by a decision of the districts, which includes the local churches. Currently, the Manual has 399 pages and their contents are divided into ten parts that are organized systematically. They include the Historical Statement, Church Constitution, the Covenant of Christian Conduct, Government, Ministry and Christian Service, Judicial Administration, Ritual, Auxiliary Constitutions, Forms and Appendix. All of these sections follow the system of articles and paragraphs, numbered consecutively.

Mission Statement, Purpose and Objective

Now we will learn the purpose for which our church exists.

The manual states our mission:

"The mission of the Church of the Nazarene is to make Christlike disciples in the nations" (Matthew 28:19). "The primary objective of the Church of the Nazarene is to advance God's kingdom by the preservation and propagation of Christian holiness as set forth in the Scriptures." (2013-2017 Manual p. 5).

We also find in the Manual the objectives and purpose for which our organization exists:

"The critical objectives of the Church of the Nazarene are 'holy Christian fellowship, the conversion of sinners, the entire sanctification of believers, their upbuilding in holiness, and the simplicity and spiritual power manifest in the primitive New Testament Church, together with the preaching of the gospel to every creature" (2013-2017 Manual p. 5).

"The Church of the Nazarene exists to serve as an instrument for advancing the kingdom of God through the preaching and teaching of the gospel throughout the world. Our well-defined commission is to preserve and propagate Christian holiness as set forth in the Scriptures, through the conversion of sinners, the reclamation of backsliders, and the entire sanctification of believers (2013-2017 Manual p. 5).

The General Assembly is the highest organizational body of the Church of the Nazarene in regards to formulating beliefs, laws and elections.

In the preamble of Part IV in the section on Government, the Manual declares once again our task, mission and goal:

- **The task** of the Church of the Nazarene is to make known to all peoples the transforming grace of God through the forgiveness of sins and heart cleansing in Jesus Christ.

- **Our mission** first and foremost is to "make Christlike disciples in the nations," to incorporate believers into fellowship and membership (congregations), and to equip (teach) for ministry all who respond in faith.

- **The ultimate goal** of the "community of faith" is to present everyone perfect in Christ (Colossians 1:28) at the last day.

Form of Government

In this section we will learn about our form of government.

The Scriptures teach that there was order in the early church. The pastoral letters (1 Timothy, 2 Timothy and Titus) show that there was an order in terms of the services, the regulations within the church for leadership, and other ordinances. Throughout the history of the Christian church at least five forms of church government have been practiced:

1. The Papacy: where the Roman Catholic Church affirms that the supreme and final authority is the Pope.

2. Congregational: where authority is placed in separate congregations. This form of government is sometimes called "independent" or "democratic" since it involves greater participation. The authority lies in the local church. Here are three truths that they affirm:

    a) The power lies in the church members and not in the bishops or elders.

Lesson 6 - Our Organization

> **Representative Government**
> Bishop Weaver, cited by Wiley and Culbertson, comments on this form of government. "It is our opinion… that the form of government in the New Testament was not exclusively Episcopal, Presbyterian or Congregational, but a combination of certain elements of all…From a careful review of the whole question, we conclude that it is nearest in harmony with practice and writings of the apostles to say that the authority in the visible church is vested in the ministry and laity together."

> **As part of our Anglican heritage, and especially our Methodist heritage, the following organizational aspects and practices have been adapted by our denomination:**
> - The assembly system derived from the Methodist conference that shows elements of influence from the Presbyterian model in the Methodist church and our church.
> - The practice of election of ministerial candidates to be ordained as pastors in the district assemblies.
> - The invitation of ordained pastors to lay hands on the new ministers.
> - The need for the office of Superintendent.

    b) The majority is what rules, the minority must submit to the judgment of the majority.

    c) The power of the church cannot be transferred or ignored, and the church's decision is final.

3. Episcopal: where authority is concentrated in a higher order of ministers called bishops. The local church government rests entirely upon the bishop who is the center of authority.

4. Presbyterian: where authority rests with the ministry and laity together. The authority in this system is as shown below:

    First: in the church board which consists of ruling elders or mature leaders who represent the congregation and the pastor.

    Second: in the elders, which consists of all pastors and one mature leader from each congregation.

    Third: in the Synod, which consists of a group of pastors and mature leaders.

    Fourth: in the **General Assembly**, which is formed of pastors and leaders representing all the districts. This assembly is the supreme authority of the Presbyterian Church.

5. Methodist: came out of the Presbyterian model, where the authority is set mainly in the elders of the church.

Of these forms of church government, the most commonly adapted in protestant churches are these: Episcopal, Presbyterian and Congregational.

The Church of the Nazarene has a **representative government**, which is a combination of certain elements of these three models. The Church of the Nazarene uses elements of the Episcopalian model (authority lies in the district superintendents), Presbyterian model (authority is in the elders) and the congregational model (authority is in the congregation) in order to avoid the extremes of Episcopalian and the Congregational models.

The form of government of the Church of the Nazarene is distinctive, because at different levels of the structure of the organization there exists both ministerial and lay participation. They occupy different positions of service and work together to achieve common objectives to fulfill the mission of the church. Laity and ministers have equal authority in the administrative affairs of the church, thus maintaining a balance of power.

This is stated in the Introduction to the Manual:

"Because the laity and the ministry have equal authority in the deliberative and lawmaking units of the church, there is a desirable and effective balance of power. We see this not only as an opportunity for participation and service in the church but also as an obligation on the part of both laity and ministry" (Manual, 2013-2017, p. 6).

The organization and governance of the church is structured in three levels: local, district and general church.

Local Church Organization

In the Church of the Nazarene, we affirm that the local church is the context in which the mission of the church is carried out: to proclaim the message of salvation, to disciple believers, to guide them to maturity and train them to exercise the gifts of the Spirit. The local church, as the visible Body of Christ, is the living representation of the beliefs and mission of our church.

Stewards: A member of the Church of the Nazarene who is chosen for specific responsibilities in the areas of visitation, finances, evangelism, compassion, public worship, discipleship, preparation and serving of Communion, among others.

The local church is organized in this way to facilitate its work:

- Pastor / Pastors

- Board of the church (stewards, trustees, presidents of the ministries: Sunday School, Nazarene Mission International and Nazarene Youth International, secretary and treasurer)

- Ministries: Sunday School and Discipleship (SDMI), Nazarene Mission International (NMI), Nazarene Youth International (NYI), Evangelism Committee and Committee of Nazarene Compassionate Ministries (NCM).

The local church elects delegates to the district assembly, participates in the selection and the ministry of their pastors, chooses their local leaders, manages its own finances and is responsible for all other matters pertaining to local church life and work.

Elders: A recognition and a permanent status that the church gives to ministers that have been called by God and who have fulfilled the necessary requirements, such as theological studies, ministerial experience, Christian testimony and service, among others.

In the Church of the Nazarene, the organization of the local church is not rigid, but instead allows for the creation of ministries and the adding of as many leaders as needed to accomplish the mission in the local context.

ORGANIZATIONAL MODEL OF A LOCAL CHURCH

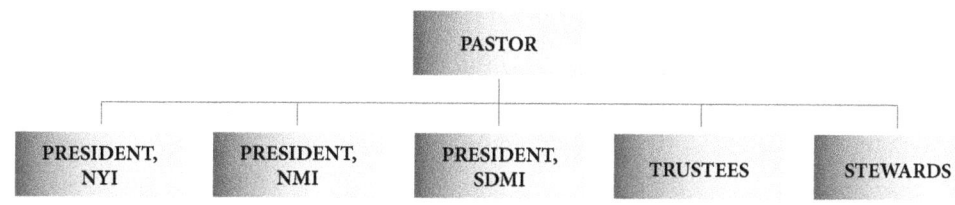

District Organization

A district is a group of local churches in a geographic area under the leadership of an elder who serves as the District Superintendent. In the Articles of Organization and Government in the section of the Constitution of the Church, it states the following:

Congregational Government
This system puts emphasis on the autonomy of the local church. Each congregation directs its own ministers. This system rejects the organizational relationship between churches and declares as unbiblical any ecclesiastical authority beyond the local church level. They have conventions and send delegates, but declare that they are fraternal meetings. Decisions made in the convention have no authority over the local church and are received as recommendations only.

Qualities of Those in Leadership
When choosing leaders in the Church of the Nazarene, the church emphases that they be spiritual leaders, that is, those who are mature in character, those that are filled with the Holy Spirit in such a way that they can lead with faith, hope, security, and love. They should be leaders that provide stability, whose beliefs are based on Scripture, who practice what they teach, who model an attitude and action of service to others, and who get along with everyone in the family of God.

28.1. We are agreed on the necessity of a superintendency that shall complement and assist the local church in the fulfilling of its mission and objectives. The superintendency shall build morale, provide motivation, supply management and method assistance, and organize and encourage organization of new churches and missions everywhere.

28.2. We are agreed that authority given to superintendents shall not interfere with the independent action of a fully organized church. Each church shall enjoy the right to select its own pastor, subject to such approval as the General Assembly shall find wise to institute. Each church shall also elect delegates to the various assemblies, manage its own finances, and have charge of all other matters pertaining to its local life and work.

At the district level, a Superintendent has a team of ministry leaders, boards and committees. Representatives of local churches at the annual district assembly elect these leaders and boards.

General and Regional Organization

At the General level, there are three important entities in the denomination, which represent all local churches and districts around the world. These include the following: the General Assembly, the Board of General Superintendents, and the International General Board. The functions and organization of each are in the church manual, but here is a brief summary.

The General Assembly is the supreme authority of the denomination. It is chaired by the General Superintendents. It consists of ministerial and lay delegates in equal numbers, elected to it by the District Assemblies of the Church of the Nazarene; and of ex-officio members and delegates from districts under the administration of the departments of Global Mission and Church Growth, as stipulated by the General Assembly. This assembly is held every four years (see paragraphs 300 to 305.9).

The General Board consists of members elected at the General Assembly, who are ministerial and lay delegates representing a region (see paragraphs 331 to 336).

The General Superintendents are elected by the General Assembly by all the elders of the Church of the Nazarene around the world. Currently there are six leaders who constitute the Board of General Superintendents (see paragraphs 306-307, 314 to 324). To better perform their functions, these leaders rely on teams of people organized into committees, departments and boards.

Regional Organization

A region is a grouping of several districts in a geographic area that are under the jurisdiction of a Regional Director. There are currently six international regions: Mesoamerica, South America, Eurasia, Asia Pacific, Africa and the United States and Canada. The regions are subdivided into fields, each under a Field Strategy Coordinator on behalf of the Regional Director. The Regional Office is an extension of Global Mission of the Church of the Nazarene in the assigned region.

The regions also have Regional Coordinators with resources to support local churches in the following ministries: Evangelism, Work and Witness, Compassion, Sunday School and Discipleship, Theological Education, Missions, Youth, Literature, Communications, and Global Mission. In addition, there is a Regional Advisory Council (RAC) with representation of ordained ministers and lay people (see paragraph 345.3).

The History of the Seal of the Denomination

The current seal was designed in 1967 when Dr. B. Edgar Johnson, the General Secretary of the denomination at the time, wanted a design for the official letters of the church. With the help of the artist Dave Lawlor, the seal was designed and appeared on the letterhead of the Office of the General Secretary. Other leaders of the departments of the General Church showed interest in using the seal on their letterhead and soon after it became available to all offices including printing the seal on General Board materials. In 1970, the Nazarene Publishing House catalog began to sell self-adhesive stamps in the gold and black seal to be placed on letters, certificates, cards, etc. and gradually it became more popular and accessible to all.

Dr. Johnson chose specific elements for the seal that had special and personal significance: The flame and the dove represent the Spirit that lives in the Word, causing hunger for God within our hearts. The Bible represents the idea that "the letter kills but the spirit gives life," and the phrase "Holiness unto the Lord" recalls the beginnings of the denomination when this slogan was used on the banners hung in Nazarenes churches.

*A **seal** is a simple form of identification that represents an organization or company. In Bresee's time, the cross was used only in printed literature. The theme "Called unto Holiness" or "Holiness unto the Lord" appeared on signs and banners that hung in local churches or camp meetings.*

What Did We Learn?

In the Manual of the Church of the Nazarene we find the guide for the government and ministry of the Church at the local, district, regional and general levels.

Lesson 6 - Our Organization

Activities

Time 20'

INSTRUCTIONS:

1. Explain in your own words the type of church government referred to as representative government.

_____
_____
_____
_____
_____
_____
_____
_____
_____
_____
_____

2. In groups of three or four persons and using the organizational model shown in this chapter, draw the ministerial organization of your local church.

Lesson 7

OUR VALUES AND MISSION

Objectives
- To identify with the mission of the church to make Christlike disciples in the nations.
- To have a complete understanding of the overall mission of our denomination.

Main Ideas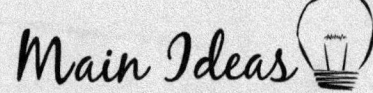
- The Church of the Nazarene is a group of people with a mission.
- The mission is comprehensive, including many ministry focuses so as to be integral.
- The mission of the church is based on values.

Introduction

The Church needs to continually remember its mission in order to not lose its reason for being, its priorities or its course. It all began with the divine plan of salvation for humans and continued with the establishment of a people of God, by which all nations of the earth would be blessed. Then God sent His Son Jesus Christ to continue the mission and be salt and light in the world, and then He allowed His disciples to participate in the mission. Therefore, in the Church of the Nazarene, as part of the universal Church, we are committed to respond to the Great Commission of Jesus Christ. We are the people of God and we have a mission that is divine, redemptive, holy, and filled with good news with a universal reach.

What Are the Values of the Church of the Nazarene?

In this section we will learn about our values.

The Church of the Nazarene is defined by its participation in the mission of God and in the beliefs and the values that reflect the identity of the Church and that are transmitted from generation to generation. These are the core values that serve as a guide, that define what we do and why we do it, and above all else, that help in the development of the Nazarene global community. The following is a summary of these values:

Values: Qualities, ideals and standards that guide a person or an institution.

WE ARE A CHRISTIAN PEOPLE

"As members of the Church Universal, we join with all true believers in proclaiming the Lordship of Jesus Christ and in affirming the historic Trinitarian creeds and beliefs of the Christian faith. We value our Wesleyan-Holiness heritage and believe it to be a way of understanding the faith that is true to Scripture, reason, tradition, and experience."

WE ARE A HOLINESS PEOPLE

"God, who is holy, calls us to a life of holiness. We believe that the Holy Spirit seeks to do in us a second work of grace, called by various terms

including "entire sanctification" and "baptism with the Holy Spirit"-cleansing us from all sin, renewing us in the image of God, empowering us to love God with our whole heart, soul, mind, and strength, and our neighbors as ourselves, and producing in us the character of Christ. Holiness in the life of believers is most clearly understood as Christlikeness."

WE ARE A MISSIONAL PEOPLE

"We are a sent people, responding to the call of Christ and empowered by the Holy Spirit to go into all the world, witnessing to the Lordship of Christ and participating with God in the building of the Church and the extension of His kingdom (Matthew 28:19-20; 2 Corinthians 6:1). Our mission (a) begins in worship, (b) ministers to the world in evangelism and compassion, (c) encourages believers toward Christian maturity through discipleship, and (d) prepares women and men for Christian service through Christian higher education."

(Taken from the web page for the Church of the Nazarene)

The Church of the Nazarene Is a Church with a Mission

In this section we will learn about the historic mission of the Nazarene Church.

The Church of the Nazarene began with a clear mission as expressed by these words written on one of the first flyers printed for an upcoming meeting.

"The Church of the Nazarene is a simple, primitive church, a church of the people and for the people. It has no new doctrines, only the old, old Bible truths…It is not a mission, but a church with a mission. It is a banding together of hearts that have found the peace with God, and which now in their gladness, go out to carry the message of the unsearchable riches of the gospel of Christ to other suffering, discouraged, sin-sick souls. Its mission is to everyone upon whom the battle of life has been sore, and to every heart that hungers for cleansing from sin. Come" (Smith, chapter 5).

The Church of the Nazarene is a church with a mission. That mission was born in the heart of God and comes from His very nature and character: His holiness. This has characterized our denomination as well as those holiness groups who joined the denomination. The mission is an essential aspect of our identity.

The early Nazarenes, including its founder, were known for their love and care for people in need. They worked hard to open orphanages, shelters and rescue missions; they aided immigrants, fed the hungry, wrote articles for newspapers that promoted social justice, sent missionaries to other parts of the world, evangelized in other cities and towns, etc.

All this was part of who they were. The Nazarenes were seriously committed to do what Jesus did, to preach the gospel of the good news of salvation in word and deed, and to testify about their holiness experience as

The year and country where the Church of the Nazarene established the work up until 2017.

1887 - United States
1898 - India
1901 - Cape Verde
1902 - Canada
1903 - Mexico
1904 - Guatemala
1905 - Japan
1909 - Argentina
1909 - United Kingdom
1910 - Swaziland
1914 - Peru
1919 - South Africa
1920 - Syria
1922 - Mozambique
1926 - Barbados
1926 - Trinidad
1934 - Belize
1937 - Nicaragua
1944 - Virgin Islands
1945 - Bolivia
1946 - Guyana
1946 - Philippines
1948 - Italy
1948 - South Korea
1949 - Uruguay
1950 - Haiti
1952 - New Zealand
1953 - Panama
1955 - Papua New Guinea
1956 - Taiwan
1957 - Malawi
1958 - American Samoa
1958 - Brazil
1958 - Germany
1960 - Denmark
1961 - Zambia
1962 - Chile
1963 - Zimbabwe
1964 - Costa Rica
1964 - El Salvador
1964 - Samoa
1966 - Jamaica
1967 - Netherlands
1970 - Bermuda
1970 - Honduras
1971 - Bahamas
1971 - Guam
1972 - Ecuador
1972 - St. Lucia
1973 - Antigua
1973 - Namibia
1973 - Portugal
1974 - Dominica

1974 - Dominican Republic
1974 - Hong Kong (SAR)
1975 - Colombia
1975 - St. Vincent
1976 - Martinique
1977 - France
1977 - Grenada
1977 - Nigeria
1978 - Switzerland
1980 - Paraguay
1981 - Spain
1982 - Venezuela
1983 - St. Kitts & Nevis
1984 - Azores
1984 - Botswana
1984 - Kenya
1984 - Suriname
1985 - Cyprus
1986 - Egypt
1986 - Guadaloupe
1987 - Ivory Coast
1987 - Ireland
1988 - French Guyana
1988 - Senegal
1988 - Uganda
1989 - Thailand
1990 - Democratic Republic of Congo
1990 - Ghana
1990 - Liberia
1990 - Rwanda
1990 - Tanzania
1992 - Angola
1992 - Bangladesh
1992 - Romania
1992 - Russia
1992 - Solomon Islands
1992 - Ukraine
1993 - Lesotho
1993 - Madagascar
1994 - Bulgaria
1994 - San Martin
1995 - Fiji
1995 - Palau
1996 - Hungary
1996 - Pakistan
1997 - Burkina Faso
1997 - Republic of Congo
1997 - Sao Tome and Principe
1998 - Benin
1998 - Nepal
1998 - Togo
1999 - Burundi
1999 - Cameroon
1999 - Croatia
1999 - Gabon
1999 - Poland
2000 - Aruba

a real life experience. Everything they did was central to their identity as a missional church (they did not limit themselves to local needs only, but went above and beyond).

Dr. Ron Benefiel invites Nazarenes to answer this question: Are we still a people with a mission? Is the mission that God gave the first Nazarenes, still a mission for the church today?

As in the past, today we live in a broken, sick and discouraged world, and the Church of the Nazarene still has a clear mission to show love and tend to the needs of the weak, to preach the gospel and testify about sanctification as a transforming, real life experience. That mission, according to Dr. Wesley Tracy, is evident in four factors: corporate worship, evangelism, edification and service.

So, it is a matter of continuing to give evidence of our commitment as Nazarenes to our mission, to God and to ourselves, and to be ready to answer the call of the Lord and give ourselves in sacrifice to follow in the footsteps of Jesus.

The Church of the Nazarene Is a Great Commission Church

Now we will see how to fulfill the Great Commission.

As Nazarenes we are called to faithfully witness to family, friends and neighbors about the transformation that Jesus Christ makes in our lives in order that others too may desire to have a new life filled with the love of God. The ways used to carry out the Great Commission are numerous and creative. All Nazarenes should be committed to the task of making disciples.

Along with the Great Commission (Matthew 28:18-20) is the Great Commandment (Matthew 22:36-39) to love our neighbor as ourselves. This is our motivation for showing love, demonstrating compassion and helping to alleviate the needs of the poor and broken as part of our mission.

Since its inception, the denomination has been involved in missions and so world evangelization is the church's mission. Missionary work is done by means of preaching, teaching, evangelizing, social action, outreach, etc.

However, this work costs money and takes effort; therefore, local congregations are generous in giving, praying, fasting and supporting international missions and missionaries so that many people everywhere in the world will have the opportunity to know and receive Jesus Christ as Savior and Lord.

Through offerings for global evangelism, Nazarenes everywhere are involved in reaching others around the world, and from the very beginning they have been generous in providing financial resources for the expansion of the Church.

The Mission of the Church of the Nazarene after 100 Years

In this section we will learn about our mission today.

In the first months of 2007, the Board of General Superintendents announced the new mission statement for the Church of the Nazarene. This expresses the official mission of the denomination: "Making Christlike Disciples in the Nations."

In October 2008, the Church of the Nazarene celebrated 100 years of history and progress as a denomination, but it was also a time to refocus, renew and evaluate where we are as a church today and where we hope to be tomorrow. Each local congregation around the world is encouraged to tell the story of the denomination in terms of its history, its message, and its mission as a denominational family.

Our history allows us to remember our humble beginnings; it is a time to renew and continue the proclamation of the holiness message of radical hope, which gives the possibility of personal and social transformation. It is a time to remember our mission to reach others for Christ throughout the world, motivated by our commitment and compassion that emerge from our core values (Grow Journal, Fall 2003).

To the extent that the church has a mission, we will continue moving forward. This mission will keep us alive and growing as a denomination. There can be no church without mission or without a reason for being.

2000 - Chuuk
2000 - Pohnpei
2000 - Saipan
2000 - Sri Lanka
2000 - Tonga
2001 - East Timor
2001 - Vanuatu
2002 - Armenia
2002 - Equatorial Guinea
2002 - Greece
2002 - Madeira Islands
2003 - Reunion
2004 - Guinea Bissau
2004 - Sierra Leone
2005 - Kosovo
2006 - Zanzibar
2009 - Guinea Conakry
2009 - Moldova
2009 - Niger
2009 - Norway
2012 - South Sudan
2012 - Turks and Caicos
2017 - Curacao
2017 - Mongolia
2017 - Singapore
(162 world areas)

The Mission of the Church Is for Everyone

In this section we will learn how to be involved in the mission.

Since the mission of the Church has been part of our identity as a denomination, it is important we know how to participate, promote and support it. One way is by knowing our missionaries and what they do as missionaries. The manual of the Department of Global Mission of the Church of the Nazarene defines a global missionary in this way: "Global missionaries have given testimony to a call to long-term, cross-cultural service, and have completed a qualified number of years in previous mission work...Global missionaries are required to have a working knowledge of English, and become proficient in the predominant language in the area of their assignment." (Definition of a Global Missionary, paragraph 1.1, Part Three, Global Missionary Policy and Procedure Manual).

Dr. Charles Gailey, a missionary and missions professor for the Church of the Nazarene, along with other missiologists agree that what differentiates a global missionary from every other testifying Christian is that they are

The Great Commission: It is the mandate of Jesus given to the disciples found in Matthew 28:18-20.

The Great Commandment: It is the teaching of Jesus about love given to the Pharisees and scribes that is found a Matthew 22:36-39.

Transcultural: affecting one or more cultures or the relationships therein.

A Missional Church:
Some Christians are called by God to serve as full time missionaries; however, the whole church should be missional. Christians are called by God to share the good news, serve others and witness about what the Lord has done in our lives wherever they live. Additionally, the church should support those who have gone to distant lands, who live in other cultures making Christlike disciples.

selected and sent to other cultures as taught in Acts 1:8. Another definition of a missionary is this: a Christian called by God, chosen and sent by the church to communicate the good news of salvation in different ways to people of different ethnic backgrounds around the world.

Missionaries have qualities, abilities and special characteristics to help them achieve the unique task which we call missionary work, which is reflected in the giving of themselves to others in love and which implies giving up certain amenities, maintaining a geographic distance from family and friends, living a simple lifestyle, adapting to a different culture and sometimes facing dangers, suffering from diseases and perhaps suffering persecution.

Understanding the different circumstances to which missionaries are exposed, the church comes together to pray and give their support. The local congregation develops activities and programs that promote the missionary work of the denomination, and they maintain contact with those sent out, and through this they learn about the needs and culture of that location. If the mission of the church is for everyone, then where does it begin? The mission begins with each one of us when we take the initiative and seek the lost where they are. The mission of the church is carried out at home, in nearby areas and far away from home.

The Challenge of the Third Millennium for the Church of the Nazarene

Now we will study the future challenges for the mission.

Dr. Tom Nees states in his book, "The Changing Face of the Church from American to Global," that the challenge for all Nazarene leaders today is to be better prepared to work in a church characterized by diversity and urban growth. To better serve in the future, today's leaders need training in the areas of leadership, communication and cross-cultural issues. They need to learn how to run ministries in different languages and cultures and to create unity amidst this diversity.

For Nees, the success of our mission as a designation depends on three important factors:

First, attract committed and dedicated people as members and leaders of our great denomination.

Second, work in multicultural teams with people who have creative, wise and sophisticated ideas, who have many gifts and talents, who have different backgrounds, perspectives and experiences, and who have different leadership styles.

Third, maintain and renew the passion to preach the gospel everywhere in the world and remain faithful to the commandment to love our neighbor unconditionally.

One challenge for the church is to learn to develop creative urban ministries to reach young people, professionals, students, workers and other groups in the city for the purpose of presenting Jesus Christ and making disciples. Another challenge is to learn to use the Internet and other media such as social networking, email, chat, messenger, web pages, skype, phones (text messages) and other technological advances that allow people to contact others in different ways, places and times to share the good news of salvation.

It is vital therefore that local churches develop a strong passion for Christ and be faithful in the mission to reach the lost, to take advantage of cultural diversity, be flexible, creative, and generous, involve the younger generation and love their neighbor unconditionally. Only churches with these qualities will be prepared for the challenges of today and tomorrow. Only in this way will churches be growing, healthy and effective in ministry.

Vision and Purpose for the Mesoamerica Region

In the Mesoamerica Region, we embrace the following vision and purpose:

Vision:

"A Church of the Nazarene that is alive, united, holy, increasingly asserting its identity, impacting the community through compassion and the love of Christ, and committed to making disciples and evangelizing the world."

Purpose:

"To fulfill the Great Commission of Jesus Christ, making disciples, multiplying and developing a holiness church according to the Biblical principles and doctrines of the Church of the Nazarene."

What Did We Learn?

The mission that the Church of the Nazarene embraces originated in the heart of God and has been, is and will be an essential part of its identity. The reason for the existence of the Church of the Nazarene is its mission.

Every Christian is called to evangelize, but not every Christian is called to be a missionary. The mission begins with oneself.

Lesson 7 - Our Values and Mission

Activities

Time 20'

INSTRUCTIONS:

1. Consider the vision and purpose of the Mesoamerica Region in light of the Great Commission given to the church by Christ in Matthew 28:19 and the original mission of the Church of the Nazarene expressed by Phineas Bresee. Then answer this question: How does the mission of the Church of the Nazarene in the Mesoamerica Region express the vision and purpose of Jesus Christ for His church and that of our founders?

___

2. Do people of different cultures, races or nationalities attend your local church? Make a list. What does this demonstrate? What does this tell you?

___

3. Explain how this cultural and racial diversity can be effectively used to evangelize others locally, nationally and internationally.

___

4. Explain in your own words the calling and the work of a missionary.

___

5. Why is the theological tradition of the Nazarenes called Wesleyan-Arminian? Also, mention the names of two major theologians.

___

5. In groups of two or three, brainstorm creative ways that your local church can support international missions and missionaries.

___

Lesson 8

OUR LIFESTYLE

Objectives
- Become familiar with the beliefs and positions of the denomination.
- Know how to substantiate what we believe with the Scriptures.
- Understand the need for the Covenant of Christian Character.

Main Ideas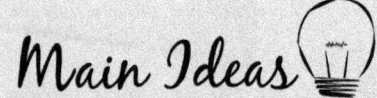
- The lifestyle of holiness is based on Jesus Christ Himself and His love for us, and that is the real motivation to live a Christian holy life.
- Every Christian should know what they believe and think (and what the church believes) and why. Beliefs are reflected in behavior.

Introduction

What characterizes a Christian? What makes a Christian different from the rest of the world? Is it enough to just be good or to do good for the right reasons? What is the motivation behind our obedience to Christian standards? Is it true that it does not matter what you believe as long as it is sincere? Why is it important to be loyal to the doctrines and standards of the Church?

What Is the Christian Worldview of the Nazarenes?

Now we will learn about Christian worldview.

Worldview is "simply the lens through which we see and assess the whole of human culture and our place in it" (Holiness Today, May 2000, p.3). Christians have a culture that is based on the gospel, and they are convinced that the gospel has the power to transform lives and make a difference in the world. Therefore, the gospel gives us new values and thus we can appreciate the culture and our place in it.

A Christian worldview includes belief in the gospel's transforming power in people and trust in the Holy Spirit to change the mental and cultural preconceptions of Christians. This worldview is something that develops intentionally and is progressive to the extent that we submit all areas of our lives to Christ so that He can change our way of thinking, our assumptions, values, lifestyles, etc. In this way, every time we change our non-Christian values, our way of thinking and our habits, we form our Christian culture.

What Is the Covenant of Christian Character?

Now we will study about the commitment to live a Christian life.

The Church of the Nazarene believes that the correct way to live the Christian life is as a result of a right relationship with Christ. To the extent that the heart does not focus on oneself, but instead on Christ, one's life will reflect the image and character of God, showing an inclination toward what is good. The Christian will not seek to do the minimum to please God, but finds that the more love one has for God, the more pure the heart will be.

The Nazarenes are guided by three principles or "general rules" (practiced by John Wesley and Phineas Bresee) that show the application of that love in the practical life of the Christian. These rules appear under the name the Covenant of Christian Character and are found in our manual (Part II Constitution of the Church, The Church section):

FIRST: By doing that which is enjoined in the Word of God, which is our rule of both faith and practice, including:

1. Loving God with all the heart, soul, mind, and strength, and one's neighbor as oneself (Exodus 20:3-6; Leviticus 19:17-18; Deuteronomy 5:7-10; 6:4-5; Mark 12:28-31; Romans 13:8-10).

2. Pressing upon the attention of the unsaved the claims of the gospel, inviting them to the house of the Lord, and trying to compass their salvation (Matthew 28:19-20; Acts 1:8; Romans 1:14-16; 2 Corinthians 5:18-20).

3. Being courteous to all men (Ephesians 4:32; Titus 3:2; 1 Peter 2:17; 1 John 3:18)

4. Being helpful to those who are also of the faith, in love forbearing one another (Romans 12:13; Galatians 6:2, 10; Colossians 3:12-14).

5. Seeking to do good to the bodies and souls of men; feeding the hungry, clothing the naked, visiting the sick and imprisoned, and ministering to the needy, as opportunity and ability are given (Matthew 25:35-36; 2 Corinthians 9:8-10; Galatians 2:10; James 2:15-16; 1 John 3:17-18).

6. Contributing to the support of the ministry and the church and its work in tithes and offerings (Malachi 3:10; Luke 6:38; 1 Corinthians 9:14; 16:2; 2 Corinthians 9:6-10; Philippians 4:15-19).

7. Attending faithfully all the ordinances of God, and the means of grace, including the public worship of God (Hebrews 10:25), the ministry of the Word (Acts 2:42), the sacrament of the Lord's Supper (1 Corinthians 11:23-30); searching the Scriptures and meditating thereon (Acts 17:11; 2 Timothy 2:15; 3:14-16); family and private devotions (Deuteronomy 6:6-7; Matthew 6:6).

Ethical Principles for the Christian Life
(from the Church of the Nazarene Manual, 2013-2017, page 46)

- The church joyfully proclaims the good news that we may be delivered from all sin to a new life in Christ.
- We hold that the Ten Commandments, as reaffirmed in the New Testament, constitute the basic Christian ethic and ought to be obeyed in all particulars.
- It is further recognized that there is validity in the concept of the collective Christian conscience as illuminated and guided by the Holy Spirit.
- It is imperative that our people earnestly seek the aid of the Spirit in cultivating a sensitivity to evil that transcends the mere letter of the law.
- Our leaders and pastors are expected to give strong emphasis in our periodicals and from our pulpits to such fundamental biblical truths as will develop the faculty of discrimination between the evil and the good.
- Christians should also be encouraged to work in and with public institutions to witness to and influence these institutions for God's kingdom.

SECOND: By avoiding evil of every kind, including:

1. Taking the name of God in vain (Exodus 20:7; Leviticus 19:12; James 5:12).

2. Profaning of the Lord's Day by participation in unnecessary secular activities, thereby indulging in practices that deny its sanctity (Exodus 20:8-11; Isaiah 58:13-14; Mark 2:27-28; Acts 20:7; Revelation 1:10).

3. Sexual immorality, such as premarital or extramarital relations, perversion in any form, or looseness and impropriety of conduct (Exodus 20:14; Matthew 5:27-32; 1 Corinthians 6:9-11; Galatians 5:19; 1 Thessalonians 4:3-7).

4. Habits or practices known to be destructive of physical and mental well-being. Christians are to regard themselves as temples of the Holy Spirit (Proverbs 20:1; 23:1-3; 1 Corinthians 6:17-20; 2 Corinthians 7:1; Ephesians 5:18).

5. Quarreling, returning evil for evil, gossiping, slandering, spreading surmises injurious to the good names of others (2 Corinthians 12:20; Galatians 5:15; Ephesians 4:30-32; James 3:5-18; 1 Peter 3:9-10).

6. Dishonesty, taking advantage in buying and selling, bearing false witness, and like works of darkness (Leviticus 19:10-11; Romans 12:17; 1 Corinthians 6:7-10).

7. The indulging of pride in dress or behavior. Our people are to dress with the Christian simplicity and modesty that become holiness (Proverbs 29:23; 1 Timothy 2:8-10; James 4:6; 1 Peter 3:3-4; 1 John 2:15-17).

8. Music, literature, and entertainments that dishonor God (1 Corinthians 10:31; 2 Corinthians 6:14-17; James 4:4).

THIRD. By abiding in hearty fellowship with the church, not inveighing against but wholly committed to its doctrines and usages and actively involved in its continuing witness and outreach (Ephesians 2:18-22; 4:1-3, 11-16; Philippians 2:1-8; 1 Peter 2:9-10).

The purpose of these principles is to develop relationships of love between members of the body of Christ and above all, with our neighbors and even more so with our enemies. Therefore, it is important for believers to learn to be sensitive to discern their own attitudes, habits, patterns and practices (cultural or otherwise), especially those that are negative; to practice compassion and be compassionate; to care for the needy in our world and those in the family of God; and finally, to nurture the good, positive and pleasing in our lives.

The well being of the Christian community is always more important than personal pleasures and habits; no one should seek their own well

Legalism: the extreme observation and application of the letter of the law as a means of salvation.

being, but first seek the well being of others; no one should be an obstacle to another, and all that is possible is not necessarily edifying.

On the other hand, believers are encouraged to beware of falling into legalism to prove that one can be good enough for God. The church is not to "police" their members in their actions every moment of their lives, but instead to inspire, encourage and instruct what God says about the holy life, trusting in the Holy Spirit's personal guidance for each person.

Official Position of the Denomination on Crucial Contemporary Issues

In this section we will learn how to deal with controversial issues.

In order that members maintain high life standards grounded in Biblical principles, the Church of the Nazarene provides members with guidance on how to live, think and act when confronting social and moral issues of our contemporary society. (What follows is based on The Church Manual, Part III The Covenant of Christian Conduct and Part IV Section X Appendix, Current Moral and Social Issues).

Entertainment

It is recommended to avoid entertainments that promote the following: violence, pornography, sensuality, occultism, secularism, materialism, lotteries and gambling (legal or illegal), all forms of dancing that detract from spiritual growth and break down proper moral inhibitions and reserve, membership in oath-bound secret orders or societies, and the use of intoxicating liquors as a beverage, the use of illicit drugs, use of tobacco, or trafficking of any such drugs.

Entertainments that encourage and promote the holy life and affirm Biblical values are supported.

Marriage, Divorce and / or Dissolution of Marriage

The Church of the Nazarene believes that marriage:

- Is instituted and ordained by God.
- Is the mutual union of one man and one woman for fellowship, helpfulness and propagation of the race.
- Is a sacred state.
- Is a lifelong commitment between a man and a woman.
- The marriage covenant is morally binding while both spouses live.
- Divorce is a violation of Biblical teachings, but not beyond the reach of forgiveness and the grace of God.

However, the church recognizes that many people go through this experience and our mission is to restore and teach Biblical principles so

How do I decide which entertainments are good for me?
John Wesley taught this principle that he learned from his mother Susanna: "Whatever weakens your reason, impairs the tenderness of your conscience, obscures your sense of God, takes off your relish for spiritual things, whatever increases the authority of the body over the mind, that thing is sin to you, however innocent it may seem in itself."

Christian Modesty in Dress
Dress with modesty at all times in public places as an expression of holiness.

Euthanasia: The action of requesting to voluntarily shorten the life of a person for the purpose of ending the suffering of an incurable disease.

Donation of Human Organs
The church supports the donation of human organs for transplantation and organ distribution if done morally and ethically.

Pornography
We affirm that human beings are created in the image of God and that pornography degrades, exploits and abuses men, women and children. The church must actively oppose pornography by all legitimate means and seek to reach for Christ all people who are involved in pornography.

that they will have positive experiences in their present or future marital relationships.

The Sanctity of Human Life

The Church of the Nazarene believes that human life is sacred from the moment of conception.

The Church of the Nazarene supports:

- The starting of programs designed to provide care for mothers and children (counseling centers, homes for expectant mothers, creation and utilization of Christian adoption services).

- The practice of New Testament ethics regarding human sexuality and abortion.

- The message of the forgiveness of God for every person who has experienced an abortion.

- Genetic engineering for prevention and cure of diseases, physical and mental ills.

- Stem cell research from sources such as adult human tissues, and from placenta, blood, and cord blood of animals.

The Church of the Nazarene is opposed to:

- Abortion induced by any means, whether for personal convenience or for population control.

- Legislation that legalizes abortion.

- Genetic engineering that promotes social injustice, ignores human dignity, seeks racial, intellectual or social superiority.

- DNA studies that promote human abortion.

- Euthanasia or the ending of a life so the person will no longer suffer.

- Using stem cells taken from human embryos for research, treatment or other uses.

- The use of human embryos for any purpose and research that takes the life of a human being after conception.

- Use of tissue taken from aborted human fetuses.

- The cloning of a human being. A human is not an object, but instead has dignity and value given by the Creator.

- The legalization of euthanasia.

Human Sexuality

The Church of the Nazarene sees human sexuality as an expression of holiness and beauty that God the Creator wanted to give to his creation. Sexuality is one of the ways in which the covenant between husband and wife is sealed and expressed. It can and should be sanctified by God, and is done only as a sign of love and loyalty.

Sexuality does not fulfill its purpose when viewed as an end in itself or when cheapened by using another person to satisfy pornographic and perverted sexual interests.

All forms of sexual intimacy outside the marriage heterosexual covenant (male-female) are sinful distortions of the holiness and beauty God intended. Homosexuality is a means by which human sexuality is perverted. The Bible condemns such sinful acts and they are subject to the wrath of God.

Christian morality and the practice of homosexuality are incompatible. However, the homosexual person needs the acceptance of God's people so that they may know the grace of God that is sufficient to save him or her from this sin and end the practice of homosexuality.

Discrimination and Mistreatment of the Defenseless

The Church rejects all forms of discrimination and claims that God is the Creator of all people. Regardless of race, color, sex, or creed, all should have equality under the law. The church understands that education should cultivate understanding and racial harmony.

The church abhors abuse of any person and seeks to increase public awareness through appropriate publications and educational information. Those who act under the authority of the church are prohibited from engaging in acts of sexual immorality and other forms of mistreatment of the defenseless.

Responsibility for the Poor

The church seeks to establish a special relationship with the poor of this world, and for that reason, the church identifies and sympathizes with them and struggles to provide opportunity, equality and justice.

The Church and Human Freedom

The church encourages its members to participate in politics and in elections for public office, choosing people who believe in the principles of the dignity of humans as God's creation, who believe in the sacredness of individual conscience, and who know how to answer before God and before those who elected them to perform their jobs.

The War and Military Service

The church is asked to use its influence to look for ways to enable nations to live in peace. The church must be devoted to spreading the message of peace. Believers should serve their nation in every way that is compatible with faith and Christian lifestyle.

Creation

The Church affirms the Biblical account of creation and is opposed to

AIDS
The church shows love and concern for people suffering from AIDS and supports programs for prevention, treatment and pastoral work with those affected by the disease.

the godless interpretation of the evolutionary hypothesis that denies that humans have a moral responsibility towards our Creator.

Chemical Substance Abuse, Alcohol and Tobacco

The Nazarene Church is opposed to substance abuse (legal or illegal drugs) as a social evil. The church must take an active and visible part in educational programs to prevent abuse.

The Church publicly opposes the use of tobacco and alcohol in all its forms and supports a ban on all advertising on tobacco and alcohol in all types of media.

Christian Stewardship

The church upholds what the Scriptures teach about stewardship: God is the owner of all people and all things, and we are stewards of both life and possessions. We believe that everyone will give an account to God for his or her stewardship.

The Christian practice of giving (tithes and offerings) recognizes that God is the owner of all resources. This practice allows the church to support those who preach the gospel (full-time ministers). Therefore, the Church of the Nazarene encourages its members to do the following:

- Faithfully tithe and give offerings for the support of the gospel, construction of church buildings, and the support of its ministers and ministries.

- Use legitimate and ethical methods to raise funds.

- Properly plan the finances of the church.

- Faithfully pay the local budget allocations, educational budgets, and general and district budgets.

- Plan ahead for donations, offerings, inheritance and other contributions to support the ministries of the church.

Steward: A member of the Church of the Nazarene who is chosen for some specific responsibilities in the areas of visitation, finances, evangelism, compassion, public worship, discipleship, preparation and distribution of the elements for the Lord's Supper, among others.

John Wesley recommended the following principles for money management, "Earn all you can, save all you can, give all you can."

What Did We Learn?

That the Church of the Nazarene does the following:

Maintains high standards of conduct and does not allow that the world mold people to its philosophies and values.

Refuses to have a legalistic code of conduct, but in contrast, provide Biblical principles that are reasonable.

Affirms that entire sanctification reflects true Christian ethics in a person's life, in all areas and relationships.

Recognizes the social implications of the gospel and seeks to develop a Christian worldview in its members.

Activities

Time 20'

INSTRUCTIONS:

1. Explain the relationship between how we act, live (our conduct), what we say, think or teach, and the view the people of the community have of us as the church.

_____
_____
_____
_____
_____

2. How is the life of holiness reflected in what we think, say and do? Give examples.

_____
_____
_____
_____
_____
_____

3. What are some creative ideas that the church, in its own context, can use to raise awareness of the ethical principles that the Bible teaches on issues that threaten the spiritual, physical, mental and emotional health of people.

_____
_____
_____
_____
_____
_____

4. Pick a current topic for discussion in class. For example: abortion. Divide the class into two groups. Draw two columns on a chalkboard. The pro-abortion group will argue first (stating that abortion is an individual decision), writing on the blackboard a list of motives and reasons for this practice in contemporary society. The other half of the class will argue against abortion (pro-life) and defend this position by giving motives, reasons etc. as the Christian response.

My Notes

Final evaluation

Time 15'

COURSE: THE DNA OF THE NAZARENES

Name of Student: _____

Church or Study Center: _____

District: _____

Professor / Course: _____

Date of this evaluation: _____

1. Explain in your own words how this course helped you to value your identity as a Nazarene.

_____
_____
_____
_____
_____

2. Mention a topic or lesson of the course that was new and helpful for you. Explain why.

_____
_____
_____
_____
_____

3. Explain how this course helped to have a more serious commitment to the mission and ministry of the Church of the Nazarene.

_____
_____
_____
_____
_____

4. What did you learn in the ministerial practice sections of the course?

_____
_____
_____
_____
_____

5. In your opinion, how could this course be improved?

_____
_____
_____
_____

Bibliography

Books:

Bangs, Carl. *Our Roots of Belief.* Kansas City: Beacon Hill Press: 1981.

_____ Phineas F. Bresee: *His Life in Methodism, the Holiness Movement and the Church of the Nazarene.* Kansas City: Beacon Hill Press: 1995.

Bennis, Warren y Nanus, Burt. Líderes: *Las cuatro claves del liderazgo eficaz.* México: Norma, 1996.
Coolidge, Faith. Esta es mi Iglesia. Kansas City: Casa Nazarena de Publicaciones, s/f.

Fernández, Mónica Mastronardi. *Desarrollo integral de la Iglesia. Curso de Formación Ministerial. Guía para el profesor.* Asociación CN-MAC, Ciudad de Guatemala: 2010.

Gilliland, Ponder W. *Credo y Conciencia (Believe and Behave).* Kansas City: Casa Nazarena de Publicaciones: 1969.

Iglesia del Nazareno. *Manual of the Church of the Nazarene 1898.*
_____ *Manual of the Church of the Nazarene 1908.*
_____ *Manual de la Iglesia del Nazareno 2009-2013.*
_____ *Manual de la Iglesia del Nazareno 2013-2017.*

Kammerdiener, Donald. *El crecimiento de la iglesia ¿qué es y cómo lograrlo?.* El Paso, Texas: C.B.P., 1975.

Knight, John A. *Bridge to Our Tomorrows: A Millennial Address to the Church of the Nazarene.* Kansas City, Beacon Hill Press: 2000.

Larson, Pedro. *Crecimiento de la Iglesia. Una perspectiva Bíblica.* El Paso, Texas: Casa Bautista de Publicaciones: 1989.

Malca, Ignacio. *Organización y política de la Iglesia del Nazareno. Curso de Formación Ministerial. Libro del alumno.* Asociación CN-MAC, Ciudad de Guatemala, 2010.

Redford, M.E. y Gene van Note. *Surge la Iglesia del Nazareno.* Kansas City: Casa Nazarena de Publicaciones: 1988.

Riggle, MaryLou. *La Teología Wesleyana en Perspectiva Histórica.* I Convocatoria Académica, SENDAS, San José, Costa Rica: 1988.

Riofrío, Victor. *Historia de la Iglesia del Nazareno. Curso de Formación Ministerial. Guía para el profesor.* Asociación CN-MAC, Ciudad de Guatemala: 2010.

Robertson, Archibald Tomas. *Imágenes verbales del Nuevo Testamento. Tomo 4. Epístolas de Pablo.* Barcelona: Clie, 1989.

Smith, Timothy L. *Called Unto Holiness.* Kansas City: Nazarene Publishing House, Vol. 1, 1962.
Stott, John J. *"La Iglesia" Parte IV de El cristiano contemporáneo.* Buenos Aires: Nueva Creación: 1995.

Taylor, R.S. Grider J.K. y Taylor W.H. *Beacon Dictionary of Theology.* Kansas City: Beacon Hill Press: 1995.

Teakell, Garnett. *Arminio y los Arminianismos.* Convocatoria Académica, SENDAS, San José, Costa Rica: 1988.

Truesdale, Albert. *Asunto de vida o muerte.* Kansas City: C.N.P., 1993.

Wiley, O. *Introduction to Christian Theology.* Volume 3, Kansas City: Beacon Hill Press: 1940.

Young, Bill. *Sucedió en un Pueblito (It happened at Pilot Point).* Kansas City: Casa Nazarena de Publicaciones: 1972.

Brochures published by the Church of the Nazarene:

Bienvenido a la Iglesia del Nazareno: Guía para Miembros Nuevos. Kansas City: Editorial Presencia, 2003.

Cuidado Pastoral de los Miembros de la Iglesia. Kansas City, 2002.

Diccionario para nuevos creyentes. San José, Costa Rica: Iglesia del Nazareno Región MAC, 2001.

Introducción a la Membresía de la Iglesia. Kansas City: Casa Nazarena de Publicaciones, 2000.

Valores Esenciales de la Iglesia del Nazareno. Kansas City, 2000.

Magazines:

Holiness Today, August 2000 vol. 2, No. 8, Kansas City, Nazarene Publishing House.
Holiness Today, May 2000, vol. 2, No.2, Kansas City, Nazarene Publishing House.
Holiness Today, December 2000, vol. 2, No.12, Kansas City, Nazarene Publishing House.
Holiness Today, June 2000, vol. 2, No.6, Kansas City, Nazarene Publishing House.

Web Pages:

Church of the Nazarene, General Superintendents, accessed Nov. 6, 2012, http://nazarene.org/ministries/superintendents/display.html

Church of the Nazarene, Manual of the Church of the Nazarene, accessed May 29, 2017, http://nazarene.org/organization/general-secretary/manual

Church of the Nazarene, Nazarene Global Mission, Accessed Nov 6, 2012, http://globalmission.nazarene.org/regions

Church of the Nazarene, Our Values, accessed Nov 6, 2012, http://nazarene.org/ministries/administration/visitorcenter/values/display.html

Church of the Nazarene, The Nazarene Archives, Accessed Nov 6, 2012, www.nazarene.org/ministries/administration/archives/display.aspx

www.ingramcontent.com/pod-product-compliance
Lightning Source LLC
Chambersburg PA
CBHW081019040426
42444CB00014B/3270